THE PLOT TWIST

The Plot Twist: Press Pause and Reset Your Life
Darlene Oliver Hightower

ISBN 979-8-218-75066-4
Paperback

First Edition

Book cover design by Khia Ancalade, Khia's Canvas
Interior layout design by Relana Johnson, Analerdigital Media

Library of Congress Control Number: 2025916336

Printed in the United States of America

Speaking engagement inquiries please email: darleneohightower@gmail.com or visit our website www.darleneohightower.com

The PLOT TWIST

PRESS PAUSE AND RESET YOUR LIFE

DARLENE O. HIGHTOWER, JD

"

What could be more powerful than owning your light and sharing it with other people to help them shine?"

DEDICATION

To my husband Larry for your love and support. Thank you for showing me what it means to be a true life partner.

"

We have to do the heart work,
not the hard work."

TABLE OF CONTENTS

" Recognize and celebrate who you are...a masterpiece."

PREFACE

The Plot Twist is for and about you. You have worked so hard and sacrificed so much. Sometimes you've felt overlooked and overworked. You may also carry a few syndromes: imposter syndrome, the cape of black excellence, the pressure of perfectionism. Aren't you exhausted? It is time to let all of these things go and give yourself the attention and focus you need. How can you be your greatest self if you don't take care of your mental and spiritual wellbeing?

Look over your schedule for the last week or month. Don't you need a break? Give yourself the gift of time by not just reading this book but reflecting on it. You go all in for others and everything else. Now is the time to go all in for yourself.

There are eleven chapters in the Plot Twist. I believe that elevens represent alignment. Each chapter outlines a key lesson I learned during my year-long sabbatical that I want to share with you. After each chapter, I've included questions to ask yourself as you navigate through these pages. Take the time to reflect on each question and be honest in your written responses. There is no judgment here. Feel free to think and write with your whole heart. I am fully aware that few of us can take a yearlong 'plot twist' sabbatical from work like I did. But I encourage you to think of each chapter and exercise in this book as a mini-sabbatical because you are setting aside time for yourself. I hope this book is the plot twist you need to recognize and celebrate who you are...a masterpiece. And I hope it encourages you to examine your own life, goals, work, and purpose and ultimately choose yourself.

Darlene O. Hightower

" Walk in beauty"

INTRODUCTION

In March 2024, I left a $300,000 a year job running a nonprofit. I was the first Black CEO the Metropolitan Planning Council ever had in its ninety-year history. While in the role, I had written Op-ed pieces, served on Chicago Mayor Brandon Johnson's transition team and was on the Crain's Chicago Business Who's Who list for several years in a row. I'd been in the CEO position for two years and I was miserable.

Before climbing the ladder to that top seat, I had worked for five years at Rush University System for Health (RUSH) running the Office of Community Health Equity and Engagement. For two years, I co-led the system's Covid-19 community outreach efforts, supplying resources, information, and vaccines to local community organizations and residents. At that time, Chicago residents in neighborhoods surrounding the hospital were dying from Covid at rates much higher than other residents across the city. U.S. News and World Report identified me as a Health Care Hero for this work, but I was exhausted.

I thought I had given myself enough time between the hospital job and the CEO position with the nonprofit. I'd taken a month off. But looking back, I was wrong. By the fall of 2023, I was having heart palpitations. My blood pressure was uncontrolled. I couldn't sleep and stress wrapped around me like a toxic boyfriend who wouldn't go away.

In November 2023, I hosted a Black women CEO gathering at my home. The irony is that we were discussing the book Rest is Resistance by Tricia Hersey. I'd read most of it and facilitated the conversation with this group of badass, impact-focused, 'take no shit' Black women leaders. But without fail, every one of them, including me, was exhausted and rest was nowhere to be found.

For two hours, these sister-friends shared stories about needy staff members, overbearing boards, impossible fundraising pressures, and the constant requirement to prove they were worthy of sitting in the CEO seat. This wasn't rest and resistance. It was super women with capes around their necks that were choking the life out of them.

And at that moment, the idea hit me that being miserable was a choice. We were all choosing struggles that were disguised as a commitment to serve our communities. As I sat there, it became clear to me that the choice wasn't between the red or blue pill; it was between life or death and I wanted to live.

Looking back on it now, I'm convinced God was watching over me because the following Sunday, I sat at Hillcrest Baptist Church praying with my every breath for guidance. And I mean, these were earnest prayers. The kind that come out of your mouth as sobs. The kind that shake your spirit because at that moment, you really need a word from God. You need to know He hears you and that He is real.

As I sat there with my eyes closed, praying with my whole soul, a voice in my head and heart whispered, 'Let Them Go,' and the peace I felt was beyond understanding. Right there, in that small church, sitting next to my husband, I decided to quit my six-figure job. I chose to live. I chose me.

Chapter One
Just Do It, Even When Its Scary

I was raised in the 1970s and 80s by a single mother on the South Side of Chicago. And for those who don't know, that meant I had to be independent and resourceful. There were no pre-planned play dates, no gluten-free foods, no talking back and no kids' choice. My mother's word was the law. And that law said you earned your keep by doing your homework, getting excellent (not just good) grades and you worked. You didn't expect anybody to give you anything. Success came from work and endurance. You had to be tough. A skinned knee? Walk it off. Got into a fight? You better win. And you never, ever, called your mother at work unless you were dead or dying. You figured things out and fixed them yourself.

Now, all of this might sound harsh by today's soft parenting standards. But I grew up in the days when Michael Jackson told us to 'Beat It' and Prince's Purple Rain stormed theaters across the country. My friends and I were built different. Working hard, sucking it up and solving our own problems was engrained in us.

By the time I was ready for the plot twist in my career, I had worked for over thirty years. I checked the boxes of college, law school, and multiple legal jobs before I left the dark side of the law and transitioned to the nonprofit sector. The idea of doing my part to help people and my community was born from that work ethic, which came from my mother.

Ramona is a product of the south. Like many families in the 1950s, she and other relatives migrated from states below the Mason Dixon line in pursuit of opportunities up North. Mom came to Chicago to stay with my Aunt Jean and her family when she was nine. To hear her tell it, my aunt put her to work. She learned to cook the minute she crossed the threshold into the house. And I mean stick to your ribs meals, like roasted turkey, cornbread, and black-eyed peas. There was no sitting around with time on your hands to dilly dally and do as you pleased.

So, with Ramona as my template, I'd worked since I was sixteen. You know those first jobs – McDonalds, working in the mall, or in my case, working summers at my mother's office where she was an office manager for an orthodontist. And this was back when they had paper files you could touch and feel.

I spent summers getting paper cuts, chatting with patients, and earning what felt like real money in my pocket. After high school, the thought of ever taking a break for a gap year, a long vacation or simply time off to find myself wasn't just a foreign concept. In my world, it simply didn't exist. You worked; you got paid; you lived. Period.

I had work-study jobs when I attended college at Bradley University. My best friend Sylvia and I were security guards walking students home from late night parties. With bright yellow jackets, and flashlights in hand – as if there was anything our five-foot-two selves could secure – we did it to help pay our way through school. At Georgetown University Law Center, I worked another office job on campus and I only got it because I begged then Dean Everett Bellamy to help me. I needed money to pay for essentials like my rent and groceries. Those law school loans only went so far.

We weren't supposed to work in our first year of law school because working could "distract" us from our studies. But that rule was for privileged students. I didn't have the luxury of a pause then and my mother would have side-eyed me for sure if I'd told her about the first-year law student "no working" rule. Sighs and harrumphs would have left her lips at even the idea.

So, I worried about what she and others would say when I stepped away from the cushy, well-paying CEO role. Just who did I think I was? Why couldn't I just be happy with the level of success I'd achieved? On the outside, all was well. I could just hear my mother's voice and others say –A sabbatical? Only rich white people do that and you don't fit in either category.

To avoid the skepticism of others and the fear of disappointing her, I jumped on a plane to Mexico City two days after I quit my job. A completely entitled and bougie thing to do. But there's nothing like good food, drinks, and culture to soothe your tired spirit and give you a new perspective. And hey, it sounded cool to say you were "traveling" as a part of your break.

Still, I hadn't had an actual conversation with my mother about my choice. She had worked hard for every bit of money or success she ever had. She earned every dollar like she had to wrestle it out of the hands of an opponent. But she was never wealthy and my job gave me the means to help her whenever she needed it. Would I still be able to do that if I was unemployed? Had I really thought this through?

To be clear, my mother knew I was miserable. We are close and there's no hiding things from Ramona. She had prayed with me, listened with an open mind to my complaints, and offered her perspective. But she knew the answers to my situation were up to me. I thought about that when I was in Mexico City and planned to have a long talk with her when I got back.

A few days after my husband and I returned to Chicago; I picked her up for a lunch date. It was a sunny day in April and we cruised down the Bishop Ford Highway listening to soft beats and catching up. I told her about my trip to Mexico City and how awesome it was. I described how we climbed the pyramids and stayed at a hotel in the historic city center where they filmed the James Bond movie Spectre. She held on to my every word and I could see her picturing everything like she was there.

After exiting the expressway, we stopped at a red light. During that pause, I don't know what came over me, but I took a deep breath and said, "Ma, you know I quit my job, right? I just couldn't do it anymore." I sat with nerves in the pit of my stomach, waiting for the light to change and for my mother's next words.

She paused, then said, "Yeah, I know, and I'm so proud of you. No job is worth your life." The light changed, and a weight lifted off of my shoulders. I'd been so worried about disappointing her. She had invested so much in me and I feared she'd see me as spoiled or privileged because I'd walked away from a good-paying job.

To this day, hearing her say she was proud of my decision still makes me tear up. It meant she saw me. It meant she understood my happiness was more important than a paycheck. That she cared more about my well-being than my money or a title. Those simple words and that kind of support were and continue to be a gift.

In those first few weeks of my sabbatical, I learned that doing something completely different and new is scary AF. You may worry about disappointing those closest to you. You may worry about what other people think. *Do it anyway.* I made a decision completely outside of my track record and history. A sabbatical was not in the Darlene playbook. Darlene is a planner, who thinks things out and plays by the rules. But I'm not living my mother's life or anyone else's. This one is all mine, and I've decided I'm going *to live the fuck out of it,* no matter what anyone thinks or says. Plus, Ramona already told me it was okay.

Questions to Consider:

When was the last time you took a risk? Why did you do it and What happened?

_____

_____

_____

_____

_____

_____

_____

_____

When you look at your life, are you playing things safe? Why?
What would it look like to shake things up?

_____

_____

_____

_____

_____

_____

_____

_____

Chapter Two
Your Title or Your Life

We live in a world where people constantly ask, "What do you do?" and then they judge you based on your response. Jobs and titles are a measure of perceived success. They give people the chance to peg you. They are boxes that come with inaccurate, and often elitist, assumptions. Doctors and lawyers are supposedly smart, wealthy, and therefore okay. Servers and plumbers probably didn't go to college, so we don't value them as much. CEOs have power. Or so *they* say.

I've seen people's chests literally puff up as they prepare to answer the "What Do You Do?" question. They are eager to tell you just how prestigious and fabulous they are. They're usually neither.

My husband, Larry, hates this question. His snarky response to "What do you do?" is usually "Mind my own business mostly," which is funny and rude at the same time. But I'd spent years building my resume so that it would be a flex in response to that question. College grad, lawyer, healthcare executive, nonprofit leader. My titles had titles. I'd earned them and thought they were super important before my sabbatical.

I'm a member of several professional clubs in Chicago. My titles helped me gain entrance. I love learning new things and these groups host interesting panel discussions and gatherings throughout the year. But they are very "What do you do?" focused. People have earned their titles and these things matter to them.

As I prepared to attend some of their events a few months into my sabbatical, I struggled with how I would answer that question. As a Black woman who did not come from means, being in those spaces is never completely comfortable. Your title gives the illusion of being an equalizer because again, it gives you the 'she belongs' pedigree. But now, I didn't have an official work-related CEO title. Would I still belong? How would I answer the inevitable question? I practiced. "I'm Darlene Hightower, former CEO of the Metropolitan Planning Council. I'm currently on sabbatical." Satisfied with that, I went off to the events.

One of them was at the newly rehabbed Cook County Hospital building, which is now a beautiful hotel. The transformation intrigued me because the old County hospital had a notorious reputation back in the day. Skilled doctors were trained there and it served some of the poorest patients for decades, most of whom were people of color. But their health care and quality outcomes were mixed and the staff often had to provide care without sufficient resources to do so.[1]

I'd worked on and off in health care for almost a decade and focused on health inequities – like life expectancy gaps between whites and people of color and breast cancer mortality disparities for Black women. So, I was curious about what the old County building looked like now with its $100 million makeover.

When I got there, I introduced myself as I had practiced. And then I moved on to talk about other things. I love a good conversation and people are fascinating to me. Some are leading very interesting and inspiring lives. But I could tell the folks at this event were curious about me. Some asked what I've been doing while on my break. Some commented on how fabulous I looked (rest will do that). And I could tell that others were still trying to pigeonhole me. Where exactly did I fit on the imaginary hamster wheel of work hierarchy?

Here's the funny thing. There is a wide spectrum between curiosity and envy. I think many of us who have worked over three decades would love to take a break. Kids, mortgages, other bills, and fear of the unknown keep us from making the leap. But I'd done it. Folks have wondered how and questioned if it was something they could or should do themselves. And that's what I heard at the County event – "oh, that sounds fabulous, I'd love to do that, but" or as one person joked "I don't know what I'd do with myself. I'd spend all my time eating and drinking…" as if those were no-nos.

In a society that glorifies and values work over most other things, taking a break feels like an unattainable and scary 'nice to' and not a necessity.

I moved on and talked to other people at the event. I learned a lot about the redevelopment of the historical building that is now a fabulous Hyatt Hotel. The floors are pristine. The rooms are beautiful with modern features and cool views. Parts of it are still undeveloped and you can see the former medical lecture rooms (or the pit as I'd called it). The manager told us that several rooms, converted from hospital labs into luxurious suites, are particularly in high demand. I enjoyed the tour, the conversations with club members, the food, and of course, the drinks.

As I left County, feeling inspired and fabulous, I thought about the fact that you can do anything if you have enough resources. The redevelopment and building of shiny new spaces across Chicago holds interest to me because I love to see our neighborhoods get a facelift and serve residents better. An infusion of capital transformed the infamous old Cook County hospital into a beautiful, award-winning, breathtaking place for respite and recreation. And isn't that what I was doing for myself? A full on, repurposing that kept some parts of the past, but brought in something beautiful and new. Except now, I was my own fairy godmother.

Not long after the County Hospital visit, I attended an event at the City Club of Chicago focused on 'the Chicago Prize.' The initiative, led by the Pritzker Traubert Foundation, invests $10 million in community-led development projects to help get shovels in the ground. But there is an intense application and selection process because only one project ultimately receives the 'prize.'

The event at the City Club included community leaders who had won the prize for their neighborhoods in prior years. It was an opportunity to shine a positive light on these neighborhood gems and development projects, while also providing information on the selection process for potential applicants.

Yes, I was on sabbatical, but I was still in these streets! I was particularly interested in the talk because, while working at RUSH, I had participated in the infancy stages of a community development project that ultimately won the prize in 2022. But here's the difference – when I worked on that project, I had a Vice President title for a large health care system and after that; I was a CEO at a well-known, local nonprofit. I had what I called 'low level cache.' Most people knew about my community focused work and knew me. And in the past, when I walked into a City Club event, I was usually invited to sit at someone's table in the front of the room.

But now, without those titles or table invites, I was in the back, in the equivalent of the church service overflow room. Because I was furious about my seat, I could barely hear and enjoy the inspiring words of the community leaders at first. And that's when I realized two things. First, ego is a thing, and I'd allowed a former title to puff mine up. How embarrassing. Second, I had to check myself before I wrecked myself.

Was it better to be at a table up front with my fancy CEO title swimming in misery because I was unhappy with my job or sitting in the back of the room while on sabbatical, reveling in peace? When I made that mental shift, it was like everything else around me melted away. My focus zeroed in on the panel discussion and the amazing leaders telling their stories of community triumph. I was so proud to see people who looked like me winning and more importantly, proudly serving their communities. Their projects offered wellness programs, job training and housing. They were making a tangible difference in the lives of others by developing projects that were beacons of health, hope, and prosperity right in their own neighborhoods. This was game changing work.

Then I turned my focus to the people at my table. Two of whom were a delightful couple working on their own development project on the South Side of Chicago and who were interested in applying for the prize. She was a clinical psychologist and he ran a non-profit focused on healthy lifestyle programs for community members. They were young, smart, and inspiring. I love to see the next generation of leaders show up as their authentic selves, roll up their sleeves and do the work to make things better for people.

I had an enlightening, ten-minute conversation with her about how doctors and therapists often misdiagnose Black kids with Attention Deficit Disorder and prescribe treatments that are not beneficial for their mental or physical health. I was charmed by the enthusiasm and energy of her husband, who talked about all the partners and programs they had pulled together for their development project. If I hadn't let go of my ego and irritation about where I was sitting, I would have missed out on the magic and inspiration that sat right next to me at my table.

The County Hospital and City Club experiences gave me valuable insights. They made me ask, "where does our self-worth come from?" Too often, we rely on titles, awards, and accolades to define who we are and why we matter. And I get that in part. We've earned those titles through hard work and financial investments in education, but when we strip all of that away, who are we really? What contributions are we making to our families, communities, and the world? A title doesn't do that. Our actions, connections to others and our faith do. I'd rather have my worth defined by God, who calls me his masterpiece. Or be defined by the desires of my heart, which are always bending toward service, community, and justice, than a meaningless title that can be taken or given away at any moment.

While on sabbatical, I also learned that a title, especially when you hold on to it too tightly, can limit your voice. We are living in a time when people are afraid to speak out against a government that is now placing politics, profits, and a lack of common sense over the needs of the people. I have marveled at the absence of courage in leaders across many of our time-honored institutions. I think the resounding silence and leadership vacuum is happening because people are afraid to lose their titles, prominence, and perhaps financial largess if they call out the biggest bully in Washington, D.C. right now. This is the height of what I call "me-ism." Some of us are willing to sacrifice the well-being of the whole for the temporary comfort of the individual.

In some ways, not having a title has given me the room and space to be bolder because no institution censors my voice. One example was my response to the presidential executive order on gender affirming care for children. I am on an advisory council for a hospital in Chicago that, in response to the order, preemptively halted gender affirming surgeries for some of its young patients, fearing federal funding cuts to programs that serve more of their patients. When the hospital informed the advisory council of its decision, my response to the President and CEO of the institution was:

> While I can only imagine the pressure faced by [the hospital] in this current political environment, the hospital's position on gender affirming care for its patients is very disappointing. Yes, there are Executive Orders that have been issued, but they are also currently under review in the courts and are being vigorously opposed by people and organizations focused on preserving our rights and freedoms. To fold before ever allowing the legal process to play out emboldens the current administration to continue their assault on rights that have existed for decades. In short, it is allowing a bully to get his way. I am a civil rights attorney by training and would not have my law degree or my life experience without the willingness of others to boldly stand up and call out what was wrong. The Executive Orders, issued without process or thought for their impact on millions of people, are simply wrong. To acquiesce to them puts [the hospital] on the wrong side of history. I would hope the hospital would reconsider its courage.

In writing that email, I could fully speak with my heart because no title or institution limited my voice. And that was yet another lesson. Don't let your tether to title keep you from doing what is right. Or better yet, use the title and your position to fight for the rights of others who may have neither.

So, during my sabbatical year, instead of asking "What Do You Do?" I have shifted my focus to "Who Are You?" and "What do you value?" Because answers to those questions tell me more about a person than a title ever could.

Questions to Consider:

How valuable is your title to you? How do you see others who have prestigious titles?

_____

_____

_____

_____

_____

_____

_____

What is more important, the title you hold, the work you do, or the outcomes you have achieved? Is there a title you aspire to? Why?

_____

_____

_____

_____

_____

_____

_____

Chapter Three
Shine Your Light

In 2012, I received a prestigious fellowship through the Chicago Community Trust (CCT), one of the largest community foundations in the Midwest. Fellows developed their own leadership programs and received $30,000 to support their plans. It allowed leaders to explore big ideas for their careers. This opportunity was a gift that has impacted my career and life for more than a decade.

My plan (because you know my type A personality self had one!) focused on the connections between leadership, social justice, and faith. Over the course of a year, I took a nonprofit management class at Northwestern University, attended the Justice Conference in Portland, Oregon that focused on social justice and faith, and I traveled to Greece and Turkey on a Footsteps of Apostle Paul tour that led us to cities like Ephesus, Corinth, Meteora, Thessalonica and Athens. These were places where Apostle Paul preached. He would literally show up in these foreign towns, preach the gospel and convert thousands of people to Christianity! Talk about leadership and faith!

I wanted to learn more about that. To somehow touch the spark of the divine and understand what was inside of Paul that made people want to listen, follow, and change their lives for the better. How could I harness some of that supernatural power to improve my effectiveness as nonprofit leader?

I was working for the Metropolitan Breast Cancer Taskforce,(now called Equal Hope), which focused on the disparity in breast cancer death rates between white and Black women in the Chicagoland area and worked on ways to close the gap. Black women were dying from the disease at rates sixty-eight percent (68%) higher than their white counterparts.

These three components of my CCT fellowship were life changing. I walked into Mary's house (yes, that one, the mother of Jesus!). I kneeled in the cave on Patmos Island where John received the revelation and wrote the final chapter of the Bible. I stood in the arena in Ephesus where Paul preached the gospel to thousands. And I saw the river in Philippi where he baptized Lydia and her entire household.

These experiences planted a spark in me, a desire to pursue excellence and make a difference with my gifts and talents. They made me want to be a better leader and tap into something deeply innate that would help people in my community. It was a truly life altering experience.

But as amazing as that trip was, it is the last part of my fellowship experience that continues to resonate loudly with me today. And it came roaring back to life nearly one year to the day of leaving my job at MPC and going on sabbatical.

The soul of my CCT fellowship plan lay in connecting with seasoned social justice leaders across the country. I wanted to know how they continued to fight against injustice despite frustrating political climates, apathy, and the slow pace of change. What kept these leaders going year after year? To me, these people are modern-day Davids fighting against the Goliaths of poverty, racism, sexism, and greed. While Goliath often seemed to be winning, these leaders never gave up. And because faith has played such a critical role in my professional and personal life, I wanted to know if faith played any role in the ability of these leaders to keep fighting for the betterment of society.

During my fellowship year, I traveled to Washington, D.C., Portland, San Francisco, and Los Angeles to meet these Davids. I also found many of them in my hometown of Chicago. I had the privilege to meet twenty-five women and men who worked hard every day to make our country a just place for ALL people. These encounters filled me with inspiration and hope.

I learned that the best social justice leaders are servants to the people they work for and with. I learned that a powerful leader doesn't have to know how to do it all herself. It is the collective work of an entire team that creates real social change. I also learned that all of them, even those who didn't identify with any religion or faith, were led by an inner drive to right wrongs; sensed that unfairness existed and must be rooted out; and believed that all people should live free of man-made barriers like poverty and discrimination. They confirmed it is not enough to point out the injustices in this world. A true social justice leader must have a clear vision of what justice means and what the world should look like.

There was a light that shone through everyone I talked to. You could see it in their faces. It bubbled up from their words during our interviews. It looked and felt compelling on the page when I went to transcribe those encounters and tried to shape them into a book proposal.

One example was my interview with Barbara Erwine, who was the Executive Director for the Lawyers' Committee for Civil Rights in Washington D.C. for over twenty years. She played an instrumental role getting the landmark Civil Rights Act of 1991 passed. She was one of five recipients of the prestigious Gruber International Justice Prize for her excellence in defending and promoting civil rights throughout the United States.

Ms. Erwine had a never give up spirit and a laugh that I can still hear in my head a decade after our interview. When I asked her about the role of a nonprofit leader, she said, "We do this work not to exercise our own power but to teach other people to have power...to empower them."

Another example was Chicago's very own Eboo Patel, who founded and led what was then called the Interfaith Youth Core and is now Interfaith America. Patel is a Rhodes scholar and was a member of President Obama's inaugural Advisory Council on Faith-Based and Neighborhood Partnerships. U.S. News and World Report named him one of America's Best Leaders and he was a regular contributor to the Washington Post, the Huffington Post, USA Today and Sojourners.

When asked about leadership, social justice and faith, Patel said: "All of my great faith heroes, even though they made massive changes in human history – King, Gandhi, etc. – they always considered what they were doing to be really small in a cosmic way, but they had to do it anyway. And I think a spiritual approach to things is to do something that's small and beautiful and that matters but do it well."

I also talked to Rami Nashishibi, Founder and Executive Director of the Inner-City Muslim Action Network (IMAN). He is a grassroots community activist who harnesses the beauty and power of hip hop culture to create social change. Nashishibi is a recipient of the prestigious MacArthur "genius" award from the MacArthur foundation and the White House honored him as a Champion of Change. He and IMAN have been featured in national and international media outlets, including the BBC, PBS, the New York Times, and Al Jazeera.

When we talked about fighting for social justice in communities that are often left behind, he said: "You can't live on a block that's engulfed in flames and think the way to protect your home is to ignore the fire around you. We are all interconnected. We have to collectively think about larger issues of spiritual justice and human dignity." Though said many years ago, the truth of Rami's words resonate even more loudly in today's current climate.

I spoke with so many others: Steven Bradberry, Executive Director for the Alliance Institute in New Orleans, Stewart Kwoh, Co-Founder and Executive Director for the Asian Pacific American Legal Center in Los Angeles and Reverend Glenda Hope, Founder and Executive Director for San Francisco Network Ministries in San Francisco. All of them, without fail, had an energy, a light and passion for justice that oozed out of them during our conversations.

Interestingly, after talking with these amazing leaders back in 2012, I developed a fictional character in my head —a kind of social justice superhero committed to improving the lives of others in his community. He was likeable and approachable with a 'get shit done' attitude. Over time, I developed a partial story about his life, struggles, family, and his love interest. Back then, I had written blogs, op-eds, and a short chapter in a book that was published but had never written fiction.

Every now and again, the character and his story would pop into my head, but I didn't write anything down. And I was too busy running my race on the hamster wheel of nonprofit leadership to devote any significant time to putting him down on the page. He sat, like a partially developed idea or even an echo of a memory, in my head for over a decade.

But, when I went on sabbatical, I could breathe. I had the space and time to think about other things besides work. Something about releasing the daily stresses of board governance, fundraising, managing staff, and planning organizational strategy helped me tap into some of the divine light that I'd witnessed in the leaders I interviewed all those years ago.

Instead of focusing on payroll, grant writing and year-end performance reviews, I could turn my attention to character and plot development, story arcs, and sex scenes. That nonprofit leader that I had in my head for a decade suddenly leapt onto the page. Ethan Li, one of the lead characters in my first romance novel, insisted on being developed. I felt compelled and HAD to write him. And the story fell into place. His family, love interest, life, and work challenges.

For months, I heard snatches of dialogue in my head. Saw scenes and chapters come together with little effort. I'd sit at my computer and the detailed storyline would just appear. I'd wake up in the middle of the night and take notes on my phone.

I'd be on the treadmill in the morning and these incredibly hot sex scenes would pop into my head, and I'd have to stop and take notes. Who am I right now? I'd ask and then gleefully write what I'd seen in my head and the dialogue I'd heard. I am far sexier and funnier on sabbatical than I'd EVER been while running on the hamster wheel of nonprofit leadership. My husband is appreciative.

Writing that first book, Twin Flames: A Sutherland Love Story, created a spark that has caught fire. I've now developed an entire romance novel series with two books written and three more in the ideation stage. I've created a whole world inhabited by these characters that could lead to merchandising, musical playlists, book clubs and talks. Why? Because I had the mental space and the time to explore parts of myself that I didn't fully know existed. I may have seen snippets of it in the past but resting and letting go of the constant grind of ambition and achievement have taken me to a completely different place mentally.

A key learning for me from all of this is that stress suppresses your gifts. There is so much richness and experience inside each of us. We hold snippets of conversations; have encountered different places and people; have experienced sights, sounds, tastes, and the feel of things. What happens to all of that?

I think there is a reservoir of experience that we hold deep in our hearts on an unconscious level that's just waiting to be tapped. It is like when you automatically remember all the words to a song on the radio that you haven't heard in years. You've tapped into something deep down inside you, a wisp of memory that comes bubbling up with the slightest trigger or prompt. We all need to tap into that. It is purpose. It is divine. It is light. But the hamster wheel and the constant grind to do more, achieve more, and have more snuffs it out and dims our individual light and gifts.

And how dare we keep God's gifts to ourselves? A light shouldn't be shielded from the world. Its purpose is to illuminate. And guess what? Your gifts aren't just for you. If you aren't cultivating them, the world is missing out. We have so many talents within us that are suffocating because stress, work and grind culture are snuffing them out. It's hard to put mental energy toward writing, or any form of creativity when that brief is due, or that report has to be finished, or we need just one more strategy session or meeting.

When I walked away from the stress of a day-to-day job, it was like a dam opened up in my brain and these characters and stories came rushing out like they were just waiting for me to shift and receive them. I am forever grateful. I have had so much fun exploring this new part of myself and tapping into my creativity.

When you are on the right track, I think God gives you confirmation. In the spring of 2025, I hosted a fun gathering with friends in my home. While cleaning up for it, my husband collected a pile of papers and mail that had been sitting on our kitchen counter for months. I didn't think much of it; I was just glad that he'd done a bit of decluttering.

A few days after the event, I had to scan and send a document for a new project. You know that analog process of printing a document, signing, and scanning it to a flash drive and then emailing it? When I looked around for a flash drive, I saw one in the corner of the counter that my husband had recently cleaned off. I scanned, saved, and sent my document, but the drive flashed a notice on my computer that the files were corrupted and should be reviewed. "Hmm," I thought to myself. "I wonder what's on this because I've only ever looked at the scans folder." When I opened the drive to see the other files it contained, I saw all the work I had done for the 2012 Chicago Community Trust Fellowship! The thumb drive included files of my interviews with each leader, pictures of them, chapters that I'd written on them, my book proposal, the summary presentation I did at the conclusion of the fellowship and even the original blog post I wrote in April 2013 about all the leaders I'd met. A snippet of that post appears above in this chapter.

It was like God winking at me and saying nothing is ever lost. There is a plan for your life even when you don't see it. Shine your light, Darlene, and move forward in your purpose because you can make a difference in the lives of others.

Looking at those documents reminded me how inspired I was during that project. It was confirmation that there are amazing people in this world who are doing incredible work. They use their time and talent to make our communities stronger and better. And in these times, when things can feel so dark and overwhelming, it's incredible to know that while time has passed, their light continues to shine through their ongoing work and the people, like me, that have been blessed to bask in it, even if only for a little while.

So, shine your own light. Find time to tap into your own gifts. I think everyone has a creative spark; it just needs to be cultivated. Your gifts could be blessings to those around you. I am confident that my writing will be a fun blessing to others because I am doing it from the heart and focused on bringing joy.

Questions to Consider:

Who are your personal heroes? Do they know and have you engaged with them?

_____

_____

_____

_____

_____

_____

_____

What inspires you? Are you engaged in work or other activities that feed your spirit?

_____

_____

_____

_____

_____

_____

_____

Do you have any ideas or projects in your mind that you've never pursued or written down? Why not?

_____

_____

_____

_____

_____

_____

_____

_____

Chapter Four

It's the Process,
Not the Outcome

Me and God have been down for a long time. I recommitted to my Christian faith back in the early 2000s and have been a member of two churches since then. When I stepped away from my job, I knew I needed to stay in constant prayer and contact with the Man upstairs.

My husband and I joined our current church in 2017. We'd sampled several churches in and around Chicago, trying to find the perfect fit. Where did we feel we belonged? Who would bring God's word to us in a way that made sense and was authentic? Where did we want to invest our treasure through tithing?

We settled on Hillcrest Baptist Church, a relatively small church in the southwest suburbs of Chicago. It just so happens to be pastored by a high school friend of mine, Pastor Adron Robinson. What I love about the church and my pastor is that both are real. There is no sugar-coating God's word. There is no prosperity preaching that treats God like a genie who's always available to grant wishes. We are to serve God, read His word, and share the gospel. Straight no chaser.

So, of course, in looking for guidance on what to do with my newly sabbaticaled self, I reached out to Pastor Robinson in April 2024, and we had lunch a month after leaving my job. I hoped he'd have a biblical word that I could hang on to as a lifeline while I navigated the wide-open space of uncertainty I'd created in my life by stepping away from work.

"I need some guidance on what I should be doing," I told him, eager to put my usual five-point thrust, strategic planning hat on to set the course for my next steps. I told him about how I'd heard a word from God during church in the fall of 2023 to 'Let them go,' which I interpreted to mean, leave my current job behind after suffering and struggling for two years.

He listened intently with a few head nods and chews (we were eating lunch after all). And then he spoke about his own journey from the corporate world to the pulpit. He gave a funny example of how years ago he was working at a church and had decided it was time to leave for a variety of reasons. He filled out the job application, included his resume and mailed it to the prospective church for consideration, eager to move on in his career. But days later, the envelope came right back to him unopened with 'return to sender' on it. The mailing address was correct, so the application should have reached its destination. But it was as if God was telling him to bloom where he was planted until He said it was time to move on.

Pastor Robinson went on to say that every time he tried to leave places or do things according to his own counsel, God would redirect him and put or keep him where HE wanted him to be. "Trust God in the process, Darlene. And don't feel like you have to make things happen all on your own," Pastor Robinson said. Simple, but profound advice.

It's so interesting how God works. My practice is to read a devotional passage and my bible every day. My journal entry for the day I met with Pastor Robinson focused on the having faith in God's plan for your life. The devotional passage referenced Hebrews 11 that lists out the stories of people in the Bible who held on to their faith despite challenging odds and no matter what was going on around them. My handwritten journal entry from that day reads:

> I was feeling down and worried about the future and lamenting the past. But I did a meditation on gratitude. It is time to finally let go of the past and look forward to the future. There is so much opportunity and God has something amazing for me!! I have been so blessed in the past and my heart is in the right place. I am seeking God. I want to make a difference and serve. *Right now,*

I just need to trust Him and hold fast to my faith and believe that something amazing is coming for me. And I won't have to wrestle with it or push to make it happen. (emphasis added)

Hours after writing that journal entry, Pastor Robinson echoed almost THE EXACT SAME WORDS to me! But did I listen to God, myself, and my pastor? Nope. I am a doer. I'm a 'make things happen' kinda girl. I was gonna network the hell out of this thing in search of my next opportunity. And for a time, I did just that. Surely, with the work I'd done, boards I'd been on, and people I know, somebody had a job or opportunity for me!

I met with everyone from my CEO friends and acquaintances to current mentors, former bosses, and staff, board members from various organizations I worked with; everyone I could think of. I coffeed. I brunched. I zoomed. I pow wowed. I applied. AND NOTHING HAPPENED. Man, what a gut punch to the ego. I mean, *have they seen my resume?* I thought to myself after every disappointment.

And then I remembered a story someone told me, that I've also passed on to others. In it, there is a young girl in a beautiful meadow with a huge net in her hand. She is literally tiptoeing through the tulips, trying to catch butterflies. Her soft pink sundress is flapping in the breeze as she runs hither and yon trying to catch butterflies in the field. She is unsuccessful and exhausts herself. Finally, when she had worn herself out trying to catch a butterfly in her net, she lays down on the soft green grass and falls asleep. The minute she is still, butterflies come and land on her, without any effort.

For months, I'd been running around the fields of Chicago with my net trying to catch my next opportunity. I was unsuccessful. Yet, over the year of my sabbatical, I have learned that opportunity moves at the speed of our ability to let go. Even when you are still, you're doing something that moves you forward. Resting, sleeping, thinking, praying. These things are preparing you for what's next.

I realized I have spent my whole professional life trying to game the system. If I just do XYZ I will get results. If I work hard enough, I'll get the outcome I want. I can make things happen through sheer will and effort. But, like the little girl in the field, God is telling me to be still. If I just trust His timing and His process, I will receive the blessing and it will be better than anything I could dream up or do for myself.

I've also learned that it is fine to let God know the *what* of things. What are the desires of your heart? What would you like to see happen? But it's not our job to worry about *how* it will happen or worse, to think we have to figure out the step-by-step process to bring it all together. Our desires should be like an impressionist painting. We outline the color, the shapes, the bigger view of what we're looking for and let God fill in the details of when, where, who, and how it will happen. He doesn't need our help.

Now trust, this is very hard for me and its counter to the entire way that I've lived my life for over half a century. According to my DNA, you don't sit back and wait for things to happen. You don't linger unnecessarily in the process. You are outcome driven. Results oriented. Impact focused. And don't get me wrong, those things are still important to me. But I'm learning that if you're solely focused on the end result, you miss the delightfulness of the beginning, the middle and the in-between. Most of life is lived in the day-to-day moments, the process. Yes, big wins and losses happen along the way. But we spend more time navigating our days than reveling in something big that has happened. Because of that, we have to learn to enjoy the quiet spaces in between.

It's like planning for a wedding. That wedding will last for a few hours on a single day. It is a highlight of your life. But the planning, and each little step of it i.e., the process, is months long and you can find joy in every step along the way, if you let yourself.

So, I remind myself -- don't worry about the how. Move forward in the now. Leverage the power of NOW thinking. If you focus solely on the fear of failing in the future, or even the highs of amazing outcomes in the future, you miss out on so much living in between.

Almost a year to the day of my meeting with Pastor Robinson, I wrote in my journal:

Embrace the moment God has given you. You are on sabbatical for a season. Make the most of now instead of worrying about then and the next thing. You don't know when this season will be over. Why worry about the next when all you have is the time right now? How can you embed yourself in the moment in ways that honor God? I don't know what's next. But I know what's now. You don't have to DO anything. Just BE.

And when I think about this year of process, I've had so much more fun when I've let go of the planning and strategizing and just lived my life. Letting go has led me to writing again. It's brought opportunities to practice law again (something I thought I was done with) and it keeps me focused on what I can do and control in the present moment instead of worrying about the swirl of crazy going on in our world now.

So, just picture me like that little girl in the big, lush green field. Frolicking, but then resting and letting God's opportunities come to her in His timing, just like those butterflies. It took me a while to fully understand, but thank you Pastor Robinson for the reminder.

Questions to Consider:

What comes to mind when you hear the word 'surrender' or 'trust the process'? Does it resonate with you or illicit a deep eye-roll?

_____

_____

_____

_____

_____

_____

_____

_____

Have you experienced times in your life when you let go of trying to control everything? What happened?

_____

_____

_____

_____

_____

_____

_____

Have you had occasions when opportunities just came to you without exhaustive planning and preparing? What happened?

_____

_____

_____

_____

_____

_____

_____

Chapter Five
Fear is a Choice

Uncertainty and fear have threatened to derail my career three times over the last thirty years. The first was way back in 1994. I was in my third year of law school at Georgetown in Washington, D.C. I had a good time in school. I had two roommates, Angela Montez and Perry Fergus, who I really liked. Angie was in school with me and Perry was her long-time boyfriend (and now husband). We stayed in a super cool duplex right around the corner from what would become the touristy U Street Corridor in the late 90s and early 2000s.

The class of 1994 was super diverse, and I never felt isolated or alone in my classes or on campus because there were many students there who looked just like me. And the faculty was diverse too. Georgetown University Law Center was a bit of a mecca for me.

I loved D.C. too and still do. As a law student, it was by far one of the best places to go to school.

While there, I sat in on a Supreme Court argument. I traveled to the National Cathedral and attended Supreme Court Justice Thurgood Marshall's funeral, where I saw then President Bill Clinton and Hillary Clinton and other political leaders and stars. And laws were being crafted, negotiated, and passed mere steps away from my law school. Cherry blossom season, (relatively) clean streets, a metro system that was both clean and efficient, good food and a strong Black culture marked my time there. It was still "Chocolate City" in the early to mid-90s.

Despite all of this wonderfulness, going into my third year of law school, I was nervous. Many of my friends had clerked for law firms or other organizations over the summer and firmed up their future employment after graduation. Not me. My grades in school were solid, but I was nowhere near the top of my class and therefore not a great candidate for the large law firm jobs some of my friends had snagged. Those firms wanted students in the top one percent of the class and that just wasn't me. Plus, in interviews, I had a habit of asking recruiters why they had so few black associates and partners in their firms. They did not reward that kind of directness with employment offers.

So, I worried. I had to take out loans to go to school and while there was a six-month grace period for repayment after graduating, at some point, I'd have to pay up – which is hard to do when you didn't have a job. By the middle of my third year of law school, with no job in sight, I panicked and had what I now recognize as an ongoing panic attack.

One night, I laid in my bed literally thinking of the worst that could happen in minute details. I'd be poor and destitute without a place to live after law school. I'd have a degree in my hand, but no money in my pocket and if that was the case, why had I bothered to go to law school in the first place? Negative, fearful thoughts tortured me all night long until I could literally feel my heart and mind slip into a panic. It lasted for weeks. Through prayer and self-talk, I gradually pulled myself together. I also met my first husband, who at that time, was a gift because hanging out with him and exploring D.C. got me out of my head and the negative thoughts. I moved beyond my fear and eventually found a job at a state agency in Chicago. I avoided becoming homeless.

The second time I experienced uncertainty and crushing anxiety was in 2008. In December of that year, I lost my partnership position at a law firm where I had worked for eight years. Devastated doesn't fully describe how I felt on the day I was told, though nicely, that I'd have to look elsewhere for a paycheck because of the economy. I put on a brave face for the rest of the day. But when I got home and put my then nine-year-old daughter Sydni to bed, I melted into a puddle of confusion, tears, and anger. I thought I had done everything right — graduated from a respectable Midwestern liberal arts college, earned a law degree from Georgetown, and made partner at a firm doing civil rights work.

Fear gripped me again. I was now responsible not only for

myself, but for my daughter. How would we make it if I didn't have a steady income? Then came the doubts about my self-worth. I'd never lost a job in my life. I'd done everything I could to avoid that fate by leaning into my education and pursuing excellence at work. Despite this, because of the market crash in 2008 and other financial challenges at my law firm, I was on the chopping block.

On the day I was let go, I had tickets to take my daughter and her friends to see the Cheetah Girls, of Disney fame, perform at the United Center in Chicago. The lights and music from the stage drowned out my tears and anxiety.

After the concert, and having put Sydni to bed, with tears flowing down my face and curses on my lips, I reached for my bible. I had been cultivating my relationship with God for a long time. Surely He would tell me something in my time of need. While puddling on my living room floor, I cried out angrily to Him. "Just what the hell am I supposed to do now? How could you build me up, bless me with a beautiful home, a lovely daughter, and a solid career only to snatch that last one away? How am I going to support the first two with no job?"

Praying desperately for guidance, I opened my bible. I hadn't turned to a specific page. I just wanted God to comfort me. I guess He was listening. My bible fell open to Chapter 1 of Joshua. There, God tells Joshua he's chosen him to lead the Israelites after Moses's death. God must have known that Joshua needed some serious encouragement to fill the shoes of one of His greatest servants! Moses had led the people of Israel for forty years. And now God had commanded Joshua to rise up and lead.

My eyes moved toward Chapter 1, verse 9, which reads: "This is my command – be strong and courageous! Do not be afraid or discouraged. For the Lord your God is with you wherever you go." In that first chapter of Joshua, God told him (and me!) three times to be strong and have courage. It was like God was shouting, "Don't give up Darlene! Keep moving! I've got your back!"

In that moment, I took Him at his word. I dried my tears and got up off of the floor. My curses turned to praises. While I still didn't know what I was going to do financially, I believed that by leaning on my faith, I would be okay. I also knew that if I was honest with myself, I had been miserable at my firm for years. My spirit was tired and I had been quietly aching to do something different for a long time.

Being let go from the firm gave me the space to look for work that moved my spirit. I had been volunteering with non-profit organizations for years. By believing God's promise, overcoming my fear at that time, and staying in faith, I transitioned to the Metropolitan Breast Cancer Taskforce. This was my first non-profit job, and it set me on an incredible path of investing in communities, serving others, developing my leadership style, and building a wonderful network of friends and acquaintances who are mission-driven and focused.

And now, fast forward to March 2024, when I left my job and went on sabbatical. The first few months were joyous. I told myself I wouldn't even think about looking for another position until July 2024, four months after my last day at MPC. And I made the most of my break early on – traveling, spending time with friends and family, enjoying all the things Chicago offers in the summer. Art fairs, concerts, outdoor dining, rooftop cocktails. I had saved up enough money over the years, so funding this diversion from a steady income was completely doable.

But as the months moved on and summer breezes turned to crisp fall days and no amazing opportunity had magically appeared, my old friends fear and anxiety began to pay me regular visits. "I'm not a trust fund baby," I told myself. "I can't afford to keep this up indefinitely. I need to start making some money. Why haven't I been able to find anything?" And, of course, I asked God what he was up to. "Hey, didn't you tell me to let them go back in November? Wasn't I obedient? What gives Lord? Where's my next opportunity?" The decreasing balance in my savings account only increased my fears.

My husband Larry, who is by far the sweetest human being on the planet, was supportive and unphased. He was clear that he far preferred sabbatical Darlene to stressed out and miserable CEO Darlene, even with the hefty paycheck. "I don't want to see you go back to that," he said, more than once.

Larry has always been super encouraging throughout my career. In the past, when I would interview for positions and fret about getting the job, he'd say "If they can't see your fabulousness, you don't need to work there." When I would rail at God for moving too slow to get me to my next opportunity or say I felt like God had forgotten about me, Larry would shake his head and say, "but look how far he's brought you already. Look at what you've already accomplished."

He is the god-fearing voice of reason that always gives me sound advice and talks me off the ledge of fear of anxiety. And he's been doing that for me during my sabbatical when I have doubts. Maybe it is his unwavering faith in God. Maybe it's his years of life experience. Or maybe God is whispering something to him about courage and what it means to support a wife whose faith is sometimes shaky.

During my sabbatical, I had honest conversations with myself about faith and fear. Fear manifests itself in so many ways over the course of our lives. Fear of missing out. Fear of failure. Fear of success. Fear of the future. Fear of other people. Sometimes it feels like a default emotion. And in some ways, our society teaches us to be afraid, because fearful people can be controlled. Fear feeds consumerism. You can ease your fears if you buy this, eat this, drink this, take this, lash out against others like this. We see it in practically every commercial or ad that claims it can soothe your current problem or fear if you just buy some product. We've also seen stoked fears lead some of us to choose fascism, racism and 'me-ism' in our current times.

But over the last year, I've concluded that fear is a choice. When I look back over the course of my life, the things I feared the most never, ever materialized. I wasted energy expecting the worst when God was continually telling me the best was yet to come. I'd be drowning in doubt and God would always offer me a life raft. Every. Single. Time. As one of my friends so eloquently put it, and as my life has shown, "worry is a down payment on a problem you may never have."

I can't tell you how many times I've sat in fear about something and the Joshua 1:9 scripture would materialize out of nowhere. I'd see it in a daily devotional reading. My pastor would preach on it. Someone would have a t-shirt with the slogan. It was like God repeatedly saying, "I've got you. When have I ever let you fall?"

And then I had to do a roll call of the valleys in my life. God used disruptions to take me to higher levels of opportunity. No job in sight during your last year of law school? Here's a job in state government and then at a mid-sized law firm a year and a half later. No job after the economic crash in 2008? Go do something more fulfilling and start your non-profit career. I will prosper you. Sabbatical in 2024? Okay, get some rest Sis because I am preparing you for your next level of greatness. I just had to have enough courage to believe Him. I realized that disruptions make space for new beginnings. Sometimes God has to move you so far out of your comfort zone that you open yourself up to take a risk—you become more willing to try something new. But it takes courage.

I asked ChatGPT to define courage – especially from a spiritual perspective. Here's what I received:

> Spiritual courage is the inner strength to trust in something greater than yourself –even when the path ahead is unclear. It is rooted in faith, surrender and the belief that you are not alone. Courage isn't just about bold action – **it's about obedience, trust, and peace in the face of fear.** In Joshua 1, when God says, "Be strong and courageous," it's not just a command to be brave – it's a reminder that **God goes with you and courage is born from that presence.** (Emphasis mine)

And isn't that interesting? It's not about having courage in your own strength. It's about relying on God's presence to strengthen you in the face of your fears. So, my knees could literally be shaking and anxiety could be rolling throughout my body as I worry about what the future might hold, but God has already said it's not about me. It's about what he will do through me.

I also think the foundation of fear is our desire for stability. We crave predictability and control over our lives. But both are a myth, especially work stability because there is no loyalty. Corporations downsize. Institutions reorganize. As I type, the current political administration is laying off thousands of government workers who likely thought they had stability through a 'good government job,' only to be given a pink slip and a rude awakening. So, if fear and stability are a myth, why not work on living a fully, wide open, fearless life instead? Why not choose to be fearless trusting that a spiritual safety net will keep you from falling?

Uncertainty curbs our willingness to be bold and shrinks the ability to envision a bigger life for ourselves. But what would you do if you were not afraid? What are the desires and dreams of your heart that you never pursued because they seemed too whimsical? Too unrealistic? I know that's easy to type and maybe harder to do. I am you. I chose law school because I wanted security, something bankable that I could build a solid foundation on, make good money, and create a certain way of life. I don't regret that decision. But in craving stability, I spent a lot of time ignoring my gifts and boxing in my choices because I was afraid to live my life out loud and by faith. Before my sabbatical, I was too afraid to take a real leap and do something that hadn't been strategically and exhaustively planned out, even though God had shown me repeatedly, He had my back. But now, I am starting to let the need for control go because control doesn't exist anyway. I'm learning that the antidote to fear is faith.

For me, this is a radical way of thinking. It requires a mind shift. It means I have to loosen up my natural tendency toward the type A personality and buzz words of – Plan, Execute, Evaluate, Repeat. I've learned that while we wish life was as straightforward as that and want to control each of those steps along the way, it just doesn't work like that.

And let's be clear, recognizing that doesn't mean I am never afraid. In these times of uncertainty when so-called 'breaking news' breaks all day long, it's easy to fear for yourself, your family, your community, country, and the world. But now, when fear and doubts threaten to pull me under, I have a guaranteed way to push them back. I think about my favorite scripture. The one that my bible fell open to on that day in 2008 when I cried out to God in frustration. I think about how far I've come since that panic attack in law school, the amazing people I've met and the work I've done along the way, just by trusting that the Man upstairs is, has been and will always be with me. I have learned to Be Strong and Have Courage because God is with me wherever I go.

Questions to consider:

When have you been afraid over the course of your life? Did your biggest fears materialize?

_____

_____

_____

_____

_____

_____

_____

How do you move beyond your fears and doubt?

_____

_____

_____

_____

_____

_____

_____

_____

Chapter Six
Fuck Regrets

In 2016, two life-changing things happened. I married my husband Larry, and I started working for Rush University System for Health (RUSH). Before joining RUSH, I led the Chicago office of Public Allies, Inc. (PA), a national nonprofit focused on volunteer service and leadership development for young adults. Michelle Obama was the founding Executive Director for the Chicago office and Barack Obama was a member of the advisory council long before he became President of the United States. So, I considered myself incredibly lucky to run an organization with such an illustrious history. One of the biggest takeaways from leading the organization at the local level and then as the VP of Programs at the national level, was how important diversity is to society.

PA was one of the most diverse work environments I'd ever been in. And I don't just mean having people of color sprinkled throughout an organization in low-level positions. The leadership at the local and national levels was diverse for the three years I worked there.

I remember going on a professional development training with my PA colleagues to New York, which was sponsored by the American Express Leadership Academy. At dinner in Brooklyn one night, I looked around the table, struck by the rich, cultural diversity that I saw. Breaking bread together were Asian Americans, African Americans, Whites and Latinx brothers and sisters. And we had a blast talking about everything from work, our personal lives to pop culture. I remember thinking *–this is how all work environments should be* – open and welcoming, where race unites instead of divides and excellence in leadership is not limited to a small, privileged few.

Ultimately, I left PA and joined RUSH because I wanted to work at a place that had more resources to invest in communities. I remember doing an informational interview with Dr. David Ansell who was Senior Vice President for Systems Integration at RUSH. He was a founder of the Metropolitan Breast Cancer Task force, where I'd worked before PA. I've always liked David. He was, and still is, an outspoken voice for fairness and justice and doesn't mind risking his reputation to push for what he thinks is right. David is also a visionary and has founded or co-founded several organizations and initiatives in Chicago focused on public health and health disparities.

So, I sat in his office in February 2016 and told him I wanted to work at a place that was resourced so that I could have greater impact at the community level. "We're working on a search for an Associate Vice President of Community Engagement," he said. "We're far along in the process but take a look at the job description and let me know if you're interested." My first thought was that I didn't have a healthcare background, other than the three years I'd spent as Associate Director for the Task Force. There was no master's degree in public health or health administration next to my name. I was a civil rights lawyer, turned non-profit leader. "You don't need to have a background in healthcare," David said. "Just look at the job."

Timing is an interesting thing because David said he'd reached out to me months earlier about the position, but we never connected. Now, I sat in his office seeking advice for my next steps and he was offering me a potential opportunity of a lifetime. I just didn't know it.

Then I went home and perused the job profile, and it was amazing. The role oversaw four school-based health centers, a pre-k to college healthcare pipeline program, a community service program for RUSH students, a new Anchor Mission initiative where RUSH would hire from local communities, purchase services and other needs from local businesses and do social impact investing in those same neighborhoods. And RUSH had engaged the services of the Civic Consulting Alliance to help launch a health care collaborative with six hospitals, a group of community-based organizations, and residents.

There were significant life expectancy gaps among Chicago's neighborhoods. Life expectancy was 85 years in the downtown loop area but plummeted to 68 years in the West Garfield Park neighborhood just a few train stops away. The browner and poorer the neighborhoods got, the higher the life expectancy gap. This was about intentional disinvestment in Black and brown communities and a lack of access to opportunity and wealth, which are among the biggest indicators for optimum health.

The goal of RUSH's new initiative was to "reduce the life expectancy gap by 50% by 2030," in ten neighborhoods surrounding RUSH on Chicago's West Side. The solutions to closing the gap were multi-pronged. They involved tackling chronic diseases like diabetes and high blood pressure, which were among the leading causes of death on the West Side, and investing in West Side communities through hiring, support for small businesses and social impact investing in things like affordable housing.

The job sounded like everything I had asked for. I could leverage the financial heft of RUSH and improve health outcomes for community residents who looked like me. After several rounds of interviews, I was so excited to get the job. And in partnership with David and my team, I did well.

Over the course of five years, and in partnership with the Anchor Mission hospitals, we trained and/or hired thousands of west side residents. We invested millions of dollars in small business grants and loans, and we committed millions of dollars in social impact projects. We launched West Side United (WSU), which is a healthcare collaborative that convenes hospitals, leverages the expertise of community members, and works in partnership with community-based organizations. The goal was to improve the overall health of residents on the West Side.

I hired the first two staff members for WSU and while at RUSH, it grew to ten people. My department at RUSH went from twenty-five people to sixty-five and the budget nearly doubled. We revamped our pre-k to college career pipeline program to make it more robust and evidence-based, which led to a significant increase in funding from local and national foundations.

When COVID hit in the spring of 2020, we were prepared to be on the ground with vaccines, food, and other resources for West Side residents because we had already done health equity work in those communities for nearly four years.

David and I were also members of the Racial Equity Rapid Response Team (RERRT) started by then Chicago Mayor Lori Lightfoot. RERRT included representatives from city government, health institutions and community-based, nonprofit organizations. Our goal was to address public health data that showed African Americans and Latinx residents were getting infected and dying from Covid at rates nearly double that of their white counterparts. Among other things, Mayor Lightfoot charged us to get resources to communities on the South and West Sides of the city that needed them the most. This was literally lifesaving work.

During Covid, RUSH had set up a hospital command center to gather data on infection rates locally, across the state and nationally, coordinate the hospital's response and resources and treat patients. "We need a community command center," David said to me one day, during the early days of the pandemic. "How should we coordinate resources for the West Side neighborhoods we work in?" So, I led RUSH's Community Command Center, where in the early days of Covid, we sat on Zoom calls three days a week coordinating RUSH's outreach programs, including combatting Covid myths and disinformation, providing food to residents in need and starting up a vaccine clinic at a school in the Austin community that ultimately provided eight-thousand vaccinations to community residents.

David, Ayesha Jaco (the Executive Director for WSU) and I sat on a Zoom call with Oprah Winfrey and her philanthropic team during the height of the pandemic to discuss community engagement efforts on the South and West sides of Chicago. Ms. Winfrey, of course, had lived in Chicago for years and produced the Oprah Winfrey Show not that far from RUSH. She wanted to help residents combat Covid in cities that had played a big role in her life, and Chicago was one of them.

There were about eight of us on the call: staff from RUSH, the pastor of New Mount Pilgram Missionary Baptist Church and his son who had the relationship with Ms. Winfrey, staff from WSU and several hospital partners. Yes, we had our data ready to talk about the Black and brown neighborhoods hit hardest by Covid. And yes, we planned to talk about ongoing efforts to educate, feed and vaccinate Black and brown residents. But we started off with a story.

Ayesha talked about her family ties to Garfield Park, a West Side neighborhood with some of the highest rates of infection and mortality from Covid. I can still remember the cadence of Ayesha's voice. This was more than a pitch; it was a plea for the lives of people who lacked the resources they needed in that moment to survive.

During the call, Ms. Winfrey increased her grant amount from $3 million to $5 million after a riveting presentation from my colleagues. Through the department I led at RUSH, we dispersed the funds to community-based organizations on the front lines of the Covid fight. Based on all of this work, RUSH and WSU received an award from the City and U.S. News and World Report honored me with a Healthcare Hero acknowledgement.

During my five years at RUSH, David and I were on a mission to serve and make things better for people. He was a visionary. I was the implementor and sometimes his reality check. "No, David, we can't do another new program because the staff is already stretched and we don't have the budget." Or "I know you want to do x, but how's that going to work in communities on the ground?" To his credit, he usually listened. And when he really pushed for something I'd been skeptical about, he was often right, much to my chagrin. The two of us, my staff, plus Ayesha and her staff, were team GSD – Get Shit Done. And we did. It was the most impactful and rewarding work I'd ever done.

But, in 2021, I became restless. I felt sandwiched between David and Ayesha. David, my mentor and sponsor, was the leader of the health equity work at RUSH. Ayesha, who I had mentored, was the leader for the community driven work at WSU. And both of them were and are amazing at what they do. It was my role that felt unclear. I wanted to grow and lead at the next level and I couldn't find a place to do that at RUSH. So, I looked for other opportunities where I could take what I'd learned and continue to do good work.

In January 2022, I left RUSH and became President and CEO of the Metropolitan Planning Council (MPC). I was the first African American woman to lead the ninety-year-old organization, and it was the hardest job I'd ever had. Fundraising pressures, programmatic relevance, staff satisfaction and board governance were all challenging. For two years, I worked to transform MPC. But looking back, it is clear to me that MPC's mission and the work that inspired me were misaligned. I'd gone from directly impacting people's lives through health care services, jobs, and financial investments to working on policy and think tank issues in transportation, housing, and the environment. All of that is important work. But I didn't want to just think and write reports. I wanted to think and do. I needed a more direct connection between my work and the people I wanted to serve. And now, having stepped away and taken a pause, it's even more clear that I want to be inspired in the work that I do. And I need to work with leaders who are visionaries with big ideas that can literally change people's lives.

When I slowed down and had time to really reflect, I thought about the highs of RUSH and the lows of MPC, and I had regrets. During my year-long sabbatical, I attended events and would run into my prior staff from RUSH or WSU. Their amazing work continued in my absence.

One hot summer day in June 2024, I was at the groundbreaking ceremony for the Sankofa Wellness Village in Garfield Park, a neighborhood that had the lowest life expectancy rates on the West Side of Chicago. In 2019, I sat at the planning table with community leaders, a developer, and others, dreaming about this wellness center and what a beacon of hope it would be for the neighborhood. I had no idea how it would all come together; I was just happy to represent RUSH at that table.

Fast forward to 2024, and the Wellness Center had shovels in the ground and an anticipated opening date in August 2025. I stood in the blistering summer sun at the edges of the groundbreaking ceremony and witnessed representatives from RUSH, WSU, the YMCA, the Erie Family Health Centers, and several local officials talk about this amazing project that I'd worked on years earlier. I was also a trustee for the Braeside Foundation, which focused on healthcare, and had provided a $500,000 grant toward the wellness center. But now, I was an outsider to the work. I felt mixed emotions – super excited to see this game changing, community development project happening on the West Side of Chicago – but a little sad that I was no longer a part of it. Still, I cheered the speakers that day and walked away with a sense of gratitude for my prior involvement and the current leaders working to get the project over the finish line.

Since leaving RUSH, I've seen Ayesha and David speak at various events about health disparities and their pivotal work to eliminate them. Both have traveled nationally and internationally, spreading the gospel about the power of collaboration and the strength of community. Since its founding in 2017, WSU has achieved incredible outcomes, which include hiring over 7,600 people since its inception, spending $237 million ($237,000,000) with west side businesses and investing $19.4 million ($19,400,000) in neighborhood development projects. WSU has also changed its ultimate goal from "To eliminate the life expectancy gap by 50% by 2030," to "to eliminate the life expectancy gap between the West Side and Chicago's downtown," which is broader and more impactful.

All of this work is so exciting, and I asked myself if I'd made a mistake leaving RUSH, David, Ayesha, and WSU behind. Was it wrong to take the job at MPC and had I allowed my ego and impatience to move me from work that I loved to something I did not?

While on sabbatical, I asked myself these questions and then I decided it was time to let go of the fucking regrets. But there was a plot twist to it. Yes, I needed to let go of the disappointment I'd experienced at MPC and stop second guessing myself about the choice to take the role. I remembered the interview process. I'd applied for positions at three different organizations and MPC was where I kept moving forward through interviews. I had prayed about my next steps – specifically that the right thing would come to me. It wasn't as if I was out here moving my life forward without checking in with God to make sure I was in alignment with His plan. I prayed constantly about my next job opportunity. And then I got the CEO role at MPC.

We often think answered prayers mean everything will be perfect. But sometimes, they are simply steps that set you up for bigger things, or learning experiences that shape and mold you into who God wants you to be. Yes, I was stressed out and had struggled at MPC, but I also learned a lot about leadership and I got some important things done, like a strategic plan and a board restructure. I met some very cool, interesting people, like Melissa Washington with ComEd, who provided invaluable support and insight. Ellen Callahan, also on the board, who was a straight shooter and always sprinkled her direct assessments with humor. And Jessica Yagan, a board member who invested in the organization (and me) quietly, never seeking the spotlight or accolades for herself.

I also had external, professional success. I was on the front page of Crain's Chicago Business for an article on philanthropy and the non-profit sector. I appeared on Crain's Chicago Business's *Who's Who* list two years in a row. I appeared on Chicago Tonight, a local news outlet, about what I hoped to accomplish at MPC as its first Black CEO. I wrote op-ed pieces on Chicago's new progressive Mayor Brandon Johnson and was a member of his transition team. Those two years were hard, but they were also productive and ripe with blessings. I still did good work, so what was there to regret about my move to MPC? Nothing.

On sabbatical, it also occurred to me that while I could and should look back on my time at RUSH with fondness, I needed to let go of the success I'd had there as well. If you rest on past laurels, it's like assuming there aren't bigger and better things lying ahead for you. You can't see the magnificence of the future if you're stuck reveling in the past. So, it was time to let RUSH go too. Celebrate what was but move forward with what's next.

The stumbling block of past regrets is a theme in my second romance novel, This is a Man's World. The main character, Ben Wallace, is a combination of Ta-Nehisi Coates and Morris Chestnut – brilliant and beautiful – but he is at risk of missing out on the love of his life because he can't let go of the past. As I say in the novel, 'the past lingered in his life like a mournful ghost. It wasn't something tangible that he could hold in his hands, but it still left an imprint—an echo—on the way he saw the world and his place in it.'

I don't want to be like Ben and possibly miss out on God's next, bigger blessing because I'm stuck on past successes or perceived failures. As one of my friends told me, "Is God patting his pockets like He's fresh out of blessings for you? Highly doubtful." He hasn't been "fresh out of blessings" in the past. Why would he start now?

It is easy to get stuck and limited by past success, like you can't do bigger and better things. RUSH was a point in time of great joy and work satisfaction, but I had to move forward. I couldn't stop there because I had higher places to go. And I could wallow in regrets at MPC, or I could acknowledge it for what it was, a great experience where I learned a lot about myself and was able to grow. I could leverage that for my next steps.

The plot twist is that you can't see the beauty of the entire view at the top of the mountain if you stop when you're only halfway there. So, it was time to let go of the success of RUSH and the perceived disappointment of MPC. There was something bigger and better on my life. Better to spend my time pursuing that than wallowing in what was, could have or should have been.

Questions to Consider:

What has been your greatest professional success? Have you rested on those laurels or have you moved on and reached higher?

_____

_____

_____

_____

_____

_____

_____

What has been your greatest professional failure or disappointment? Have you allowed it to hold you back from greater things? Why?

_____

_____

_____

_____

_____

_____

_____

_____

Me and Larry, Turks and Caicos
November 2024

Mom, Me and Sydni, Turks and
Caicos, November 2024

Mom and Sydni, Turks and Caicos,
November 2024

Me and Dr. David Ansell, Community Service Event, Summer 2020

Me, Sydni, Morris Chestnut, Harold Perrineau, Sable Bourbon Meet and Greet, Chicago, February 2025

Me and Sylvia, Kaytranada Concert, Chicago, July 2024

The Lovelies, March 2025

Chapter Seven
Find and Love Your People

My mother is in her seventies. It's interesting when your parents get older. They morph from being the masters of your universe as a child to ordinary human beings with flaws and frailties. Ms. Ramona was a titan during my childhood. She was strict and kept me on a short leash. There would be no shenanigans when I was a kid – like late night high school parties, boys coming over to the house or even going outside uncoiffed. Hair had to be together. Nails done. Diction tight. Because I was an extension of her. Her stature was five feet, but her presence in my life growing up was ten feet tall.

But like many people her age, my mother has struggled with chronic disease. Things like high blood pressure and diabetes have nipped at her heels for years like a pack of wild dogs. Sometimes she was yards ahead, other times they'd overtake her. I knew she was working on her health challenges, but my knowledge was at a distance – like a distant relative. You know they exist, but you don't have to deal with them every day, up close and personal, so you don't know the details.

For years, she had needed a surgical procedure. Over time, her symptoms became worse, and they started to affect the quality of her life. She talked to me about it occasionally, but I was deep in the throes of several high stress, high-impact jobs, one of which was in healthcare. I was so focused on the day-to-day grind of my work that I didn't delve more closely into my mother's health challenges. What I did know is that she could not get the procedure done that she needed because she has diabetes and her A1C, or 'sugar' levels were off the charts. Bodies don't heal well when diabetes is uncontrolled, and no doctor would take the risk of doing my mother's surgery under those circumstances.

The health care industry is interesting. Hospitals often have doctors with vastly different life experiences than the patients they treat. And those differences sometimes breed judgment. So, it was very easy for some of my mother's doctors to criticize her for the elevated A1C numbers without offering a full plan for her to get better. And they hadn't bothered to really get to know my mother and her life circumstances. They saw a number on a chart and judged accordingly.

She would tell me about those experiences, and I sympathized. But, because of the demands of my jobs, I wasn't in the room to hear the doctors' words, see the criticism on their faces, or see my mother curl in on herself from their lack of bedside manner. Ramona was a titan when I was a kid, but now she was an elderly Black woman on Medicare in those spaces. Those demographics made her vulnerable to a healthcare system that often respects neither.

But guess what? Newly liberated from my full-time job, I had all the time in the world to get involved. And I had nearly ten years of experience working in the healthcare. So, I started going to her primary care and OB/GYN appointments which, of course, were in two different locations. I'd pick her up from her house and we'd head to the doctor's office.

Her A1C levels remained high, even though she was on medication. How was that possible? What's the point of taking medicine if it doesn't address the ailment it's supposed to manage or fix? The high sugar levels meant she couldn't have the surgery.

During one of her doctor's visits in June 2024, the physician went over my mother's list of medications and tutted about the A1C blood test results. "Why isn't she on Ozempic?" I asked the doctor. "I know that works well to lower A1C levels. She really wants to get her levels down so she can have the surgery. It's been years now."

I don't remember the explanation for her NOT being on it, but this seemed like a no-brainer to me. Why hadn't they offered it as a viable option? By being in the room and pushing, they put her on the medication. Within a few months, her A1C level went from 8.9 to 5.6., which was one click above normal. She was now eligible for the surgery. To be clear, my mother went on a four-year journey trying to get her blood sugar levels under control and have the surgery done. Four years! And now, with just a little bit of advocacy on her behalf, she had access to game-changing medication.

But through a series of delays on the hospital's part and her part, the doctors pushed the surgery back to the second week of December 2024. Still, she was excited. Now she could get back to living her life pain free. She'd had a few follow-up visits and tests to prepare for the surgery and again, I'd gone with her because my schedule was wide open.

On December 16, 2024, the day of the surgery, I picked her up from her house and we traveled to the hospital. She was excited and understandably nervous. But all was not well. When we arrived there, I got a phone call from a nurse. They couldn't do the surgery because the A1C test results were too old. The doctors did the test over the summer and it was now the end of the year. My mother would need to have her blood drawn again to make sure her diabetes was still controlled. And of course, she'd have to schlep halfway across the huge and complex hospital campus to get that done. It was noon when I got the call. They'd scheduled her surgery for 1 p.m.

"What?!" I said to the nurse. "We were just at the hospital last week to get other tests done to prep for the surgery. Why didn't someone mention it then?" No explanation. "Can we just rely on the prior results? You want me to hustle my seventy-four-year-old mother halfway across campus for a blood draw when you could have done the test last week?" Yes. Oh, I was hot. I got even angrier when they tried to blame my mother for the lapsed test. I nice/nastily let the nurse know I was not pleased.

An hour and a half later, after they'd done the test and my mother was in the pre-surgery room, the surgeon came in to go over the procedure. My mother is a small woman. And laying in that hospital bed, tucked in under the covers, she looked even tinier. The surgeon brought up the missing blood test again and made it seem like she had done something wrong that caused the surgery to be delayed.

At that point, I snapped and the surgeon was not ready. I used every bit of those bachelors and juris doctor degrees to advocate for my mother. She is five feet tall and one hundred and twenty pounds, but my voice was a giant in that room. I'm not a doctor, but I'm an expert at pushing back on people and systems that try to make me and my mother feel small. Not that day and not on my watch.

I told the surgeon about our prior doctor's visits and tests taken just a few days earlier. I questioned why they didn't include the A1C blood draw in the surgery preparation at that time. I let him know it was inconvenient and ridiculous to call my mother an hour before the surgery to get the test done and require her to walk nearly half a mile to another part of the campus. This wasn't her fault. It was theirs. Seeing my face and hearing my voice made a difference. He apologized right then. And hours later, after the successful surgery, he apologized again for the mix up.

I was at the hospital for nearly twelve hours that day. She doesn't know it, but I slipped into her recovery room while she was asleep, just to confirm they were keeping her overnight and to make sure she was okay. I wouldn't have been able to do any of that if I had been stressed about making it into the office the next morning.

Dividing your time between family needs and work obligations can be super stressful. And there have certainly been times when I've chosen the latter over the former, for a variety of reasons. Fortunately, I didn't have to make that difficult choice and ultimately, my mother did well with the surgery and is well now.

I tell this story because it's about being present for the people you love. There is something about just showing the hell up. Not chatting by Face Time or texting. Not just sending money or giving gifts. But gracing the people you love with your presence. Seeing them in three-D is so important.

Taking a pause from work gave me time to spend with my mother. I had space on my calendar to walk with her on her health journey with various doctors and institutions. I could stand in the gap between her and a health system that can be frustrating and lack compassion. I embraced the truth that my relationship with her is too important to engage in it from a distance.

And over the course of the year, there were many instances like that when I had more than enough time to spend with loved ones up close. Picking my daughter Sydni up from the airport in the middle of the day after one of her life changing or fun trips. "Mom, I have tea," she'd say. And I was there to listen and sip every drop. Or having her come by my house on work from home days where we could sit at the dining room table, do work and talk about everything from navigating office culture to the bigger dreams of her career. I could offer advice to her face to face instead of by text or after hours when I'd be too tired to engage deeply. Being present to witness the roses and thorns of her life firsthand has been a blessing.

My daughter has even become one of my running buddies and she is super entertaining. She is always down for my shenanigans and sometimes pushes me to frolic more than I intend to. Meeting 1990s sex symbol Morris Chestnut from Boys in the Hood and The Best Man movies is just one example. Morris is an icon in Black culture.

In my head, the main character Ben Wallace in my second romance novel, This is a Man's World, resembles Mr. Chestnut. Sydni is aware of this, having read the first draft of the book. Late one evening, I got a text from her that Morris was coming to Chicago to promote his new Sable Bourbon brand at the Binny's Depot liquor (Binny's) store. "We should go," she said, sending the link for the event. I dashed off a quick "Yep" in response.

I got so caught up in seeing him in person and spending time with Sydni that I forgot I had a board meeting for City Colleges of Chicago (CCC) that same day and that it would end close to the time we planned to be at Binny's. Of course, the meeting was on the other side of town and Chicago traffic during rush hour is not for the faint of heart.

After the CCC board meeting, I got into my car, looked at the thick traffic, and called Sydni. "I'm not going to make it in time. This traffic is terrible, plus I'm tired. It's been a long day." "Ma, come on," she said. "He's in Chicago, only thirty minutes away from where you are right now. There's no reason why we shouldn't be there. You don't want to miss this." She was right. And the expressway gods must have heard her because the roads opened up like the parting of the Red Sea. Before I knew it, I was at Binny's, in line with her and ready to see Morris.

We had a time! Chatting with other people in line. Checking out the crowd and their fashions. Wondering how tall Morris would be. And bonus! Harold Perrineau, also from The Best Man movies and the hit TV series From, would also be there. We learned this from another patron while standing in line waiting for the event to start. Harold is also an investor in Sable Bourbon, along with Taye Diggs. Again, these men are beloved in Black culture.

After standing in line for about an hour, we were ready for our close ups. And I'm so glad I listened to Sydni and made it to the event. Morris and Harold were both gracious as we chatted during our brief photo op. And they looked just as good in person as they do on TV and IG! Especially Morris, who is definitely Ben Wallace in my book. Seeing him in person confirmed it! Sydni posted our photo with Morris and Harold on IG and it became part of Harold's reel from the Chicago event. We were IG famous for about ten minutes!

Making time to spend with my daughter and doing something frivolous, like a photo op with a celebrity (a fine celebrity, but I digress) was both fun and memorable. Our joy meters were on ten that day. And it reaffirmed the importance of making time for family and community. It doesn't have to be something major, like a wedding or a graduation. It could be something as simple as an event with a celebrity crush.

Sydni and I have had other adventures during my sabbatical. Like going to concerts with her and my best friend Sylvia. We snagged tickets to see Missy Elliott and dance music D.J./producer Kaytranada in July and August 2024. Both of them are multi-Grammy Award winners. Best.Concerts.Ever.

One thing I loved about Kaytranada's concert was the crowd. The ages ranged from late teens to people in their fifties. And he attracted a diverse fanbase. Every color of the rainbow was at that concert looking 'fresh to death.' The concert was outdoors and the weather along Lake Michigan was magical as me, Sydni and Sylvia snapped our fingers, wiggled our shoulders, and swayed our hips to soulful dance beats. I haven't danced that hard for that long since college. I had over 20,000 steps that day, which matters for us women of a certain age.

Missy Elliott is a musical genius and visionary. Her concert took us way back to the lyrical jams, creative visuals, and beats of the early 2000s. Hearing my daughter sing the words to Missy's songs confirmed she was raised right. And seeing the joy on her and Sylvia's faces as they jammed to Missy's hip hop beats was soul satisfying. Again, our joy meters were on ten!

I've also been able to fellowship with other leaders and acquaintances while on sabbatical. Like having lunch with Colleen Connell, the Executive Director of the American Civil Liberties Union and talking about things other than the frustrating state of our democracy. Instead, we consoled and lifted each other up through laughter and stories about our families and my sabbatical.

I traveled with my husband Larry to Mexico City for the first time, and to Montreal for their annual summer jazz festival, experiencing a different pace of life and feelings of belonging in both cities. While in Montreal, it was so magical to see diverse faces across the African diaspora and hear French spoken by so many people of color. I'm teaching myself French, so it was very cool to be surrounded by that language.

I also went to Turks and Caicos with Larry, Sydni, and my mother to celebrate milestone birthdays – twenty-five for Sydni; seventy-five for my mom. We have never traveled together as a family, so this was something new for us that ultimately turned out to be lovely. One thing I appreciated the most was seeing how happy my mother was just being there. Traveling to the Turks was on her bucket list and it was so rewarding to be a part of fulfilling that goal.

As I look back on these adventures, I know I was fully present with the people I love. I wasn't checking e-mails, coordinating calendars and schedules, or planning for the next day of work. I didn't have to step away from my family to take work calls. My eyes, mind, heart, and body were with my loved ones in every moment. What an extraordinary gift.

The plot twist of my sabbatical gave me time and space for friends, family, and acquaintances. I've learned even more that building community and making connection is central to my overall well-being. I think our spirits crave connection. I know I do. But you need time for it to be meaningful. Trying to squeeze in authentic connections with my network of loved ones on a weekend alone, or while juggling a stressful job, is really hard. And because of that, being fully present rarely happened. But with my schedule more open, I filled the spaces with the people I love the most.

The time we spent in social isolation during the Covid pandemic should have taught us the lesson about the critical need for social connection. But, somehow, we missed it. Instead of acknowledging the power of community and the importance of coming together, we have dissolved into a state of 'me-ism.' But I am convinced you will never be completely happy or fulfilled doing things solely by and for yourself. Life is a group project. It just is. And we are better off as a community and society accepting that and making the most of the time we have with each other.

Even God had Jesus and the Holy Spirit as his companions. Abram, was also a friend of God. Jesus rocked with a whole crew! He rolled deep with the twelve apostles. Are you better or more knowledgeable than God when it comes to the need for community? If community was good enough for God, it should be good enough for all of us.

As I write this in the early spring of 2025, my mother has already had her post surgery, primary care checkups. I went with her for the doctor's visit. Her A1C levels are perfect. She is in good health and good spirits. During her last visit, we talked and laughed while we waited for the doctor to come in. "I hope they don't come in here telling me something else is wrong," she joked. "Every time I come here my blood pressure goes up." *Don't worry, I've got your back,* I thought. I am here. I am fully present. And nobody's gonna mess with my momma.

Questions to consider:

Who is in your friend circle and how often do you spend time with them? Are you intentional about spending time with those who are close to you?

_____

_____

_____

_____

_____

_____

When was the last time you did something frivolous just for fun? Why has it been so long?

_____

_____

_____

_____

_____

_____

_____

Think about the last concert, exhibit or event that brought you joy. How can you curate experiences like that more often?

_____

_____

_____

_____

_____

_____

_____

_____

Chapter Eight
Our Lifestyles are Killing Us

Work will stress you out. Especially if you're a leader trying to make your community, city, country, or the world a better place. And in this country, that, and pursuing success and money on the never-ending hamster wheel, has our stress levels at their highest peak. We applaud grind culture and side hustles. Jobs think they are doing you a favor by offering three weeks of vacation out of a fifty-two-week year. WTF? And we've bought into the idea that working hard is synonymous with success. This is especially true for Black folks.

How many of us have been told you have to work twice as hard to get half as far? I've always hated that expression, while understanding the idea behind it – that Black folks have to work harder than others for every bit of success we achieve. But grinding, hustling, and baptizing ourselves in stress causes serious health problems. Stress is linked to high blood pressure, diabetes, and heart attacks.

In a 2023 study by the Washington Area Women's Foundation in D.C., 90% of the Black Women leaders surveyed expressed that their occupations had detrimental effects on their health and well-being, manifesting as chronic stress, fatigue, elevated blood pressure, and impacts on mental health.[2] A significant majority of these leaders also stated that sabbaticals could be helpful for their overall well-being.

In the early fall of 2023, my 'get shit done' default mode, type A personality and perfectionist tendencies had become the primordial soup for poor health. In trying to transform an organization, I had allowed stress to negatively impact my physical and mental wellbeing. And I couldn't understand it. I worked out four times a week. I prayed and meditated. I ate reasonably well.

But during a doctor's visit that fall, and after getting blood work done, my A1C level was at 6.0, meaning I was pre-diabetic. My blood pressure was uncontrolled, despite being on medication. And I couldn't lose weight no matter how hard I tried. Side bar: I'm convinced the scales at the doctor's office are spawns of the devil because they always add five to seven pounds more weight on me than my scale at home. But I digress. My point is that, despite doing things that should have led to optimum health, stress had negated all of my efforts.

I was also angry. The slightest things could set me off. Cut me off in traffic? A slew of obscenities flew out of my mouth. Say something that hits me the wrong way? My face immediately showed my displeasure because I am and will never be a poker player. I was snappy at home, at the office, in the grocery store, everywhere.

In the first few weeks of my sabbatical, I couldn't shake my anger. I had removed myself from a stressful environment, but I wore stress like a tattoo. In an effort to relax, I planned a trip to the Art Institute of Chicago. I was excited because there's something about the impressionists paintings there, in particular those done by Monet, that calm me. I can sit for an hour just watching how the light catches Monet's haystack paintings or the ones of the Houses of Parliament. I've even seen paintings in his series called "Mist" that are so beautiful, it's hard not to smile when you look at them. So surely, Monet would be the antidote to my ongoing anger and irritation. And sure enough, those paintings were just as beautiful during my visit to the Art Institute as they were over a hundred years ago when Monet painted them.

But the anger caused by my stress was just as persistent. After seeing the paintings, I grabbed a coffee and a pastry at one of the cafés inside the museum. Both were relatively packed, and I was excited to snag a table. I took up one of the four seats. As I perused through a museum pamphlet, an older white woman cautiously approached and asked if she and her companion could share my table.

Without hesitation, I snarled at the poor woman and said "No!" Given the look of fear on her face, I'm sure I probably looked like I had a shank in my hand ready to strike. I felt bad and tried to offer up the seats, but by then it was too late. She'd scurried away.

Now, why had I lashed out? I could argue I'd been angry at the white woman's sense of entitlement. Why was she asking to sit at my table? Haven't Black folks given up enough? LOL. Chill out Harriet, there's no need for an underground railroad here. I could argue she'd just caught me off guard and I said the first thing that came to mind. But even if that was true, my response was rude. I could argue I was having a bad day, but that wasn't true either; I'd just walked through the beautiful Impressionists exhibit.

When I thought about it while going home (yes, I was still feeling bad), I concluded that lingering stress had morphed into an anger I couldn't shake. It was like being a fully stretched rubber band ready to pop at any moment. That boiling in the pit of your stomach, that tension that pulses through your head, the way you hold your body tight to either protect or soothe, is not natural. It is the absolute opposite of what optimum health looks like.

But for many of us, our jobs and work produce these physical responses every single day. Short deadlines, irritating staff, funding pressures, and the feeling that there is never enough time in the day to do what needs to be done have simply stressed us out. Our health, joy, and happiness have suffered the consequences. We have suffered the consequences, and it's not good.

Rest is an important thing. And I don't just mean physical rest. I mean taking a mental step back from constant problem solving, strategizing, responding, fixing, and doing – all the time. When do you give yourself a chance to just be and breathe? I don't think we realize how tired and stressed we all really are because we don't take breaks. I have friends who literally work on vacation. Why are we doing that to ourselves? Who benefits from your never-ending diligence? Certainly not you. And the folks you're working for and with don't appreciate it anyway.

Some of us, especially Black women (yes, I'm calling us out), feel like we have to save everything and everybody. We put on our super woman capes as if it's our job to save the day ... every day. We applaud over work, 'get it done' mantras and 'we making things happen' perspectives. I know because I did it too. But we wear ourselves out. I am done trying to save people, places and things that either don't want to be helped or refuse to help themselves. I believe in collective work and collaboration, not being sacrificed on the cross like Jesus.

Within a month of leaving MPC, I'd lost weight without even trying. It's like the stress had packed on weight despite me working out and constantly being on some kind of program. That stress weight just released itself. And I no longer had that Sunday morning anxiety in my stomach just thinking about the week ahead.

As my time off progressed, I thought about ways to prolong that stress relief and joy. I even adopted the word joy to kick off 2025. How could I live my life differently? How could I develop tools to wrangle stress in the future?

I know you can't completely avoid stress because we are living imperfect lives in an imperfect world where we don't always control what's going on around us. But like most things, I think there is a spectrum that goes from stress-free to stressed out. I want to be closer to the left side of the pendulum than the right and I rebuke any person, place, or thing that leads me back to my pre-sabbatical, stressed out self. I am a different person now and people can see it. I can't tell you how many times over the last year I've been told I'm glowing or seem more relaxed.

Here's the plot twist on how I've created more peace and less stress in my life:

A)	Travel – Take the damn trip! Some of you are sitting on paid time off and vacation days like there's an award for working yourself to death. There isn't and that to do list and workload will still be there no matter how many hours you work per day anyway. So, take your well-deserved break. And sometimes you need to go by yourself. Group travel is great, but it requires coordinating schedules with busy people. You'll never make it.

In June 2024, I took myself to New York city. My plan was to take an in-studio Peloton class (yeah, I'm a part of that 'cult') but when it was cancelled a few days before I was supposed to go, I took the trip anyway. And I had a time! I went to the Guggenheim museum, where I discovered I don't like or understand modern art (at least now I know). I saw my first Broadway Show –Alicia Keys' Hell's Kitchen—and it was FANTASTIC! It was a love fest to her music, and I sang every note (off key) that I could remember; and I ate great food, of note was Bangkok Supper Club. The food melted in my mouth. Traveling alone gave me time to stop and reflect on my own schedule without coordinating with other people.

> B)   Stop Dieting – Eat the cookie and have the cocktail. I've lost and gained the same twenty pounds for twenty years. I've done every weight loss program ever created. Weight Watchers, intermittent fasting, Forty Day Turn Up, Create My Weight, fasting, purging. You name it, I've tried it. I'd look in the mirror and think – if I could just lose these twenty pounds, all would be right with the world. No, Sis, it won't. It wasn't when you lost the weight the last time. And even if it disappeared like magic tomorrow, you'd find something else to lament and criticize yourself about.

Toward the end of my sabbatical, I just decided to let it go and focus on my overall well-being. I will NEVER do another weight loss program or diet again. They just don't stick for me. Instead, I will keep things simple. Drink more water. Move my body. Eat lots of vegetables and protein. Feed my spirit with joy, light, and peace. But your girl loves a good cocktail and a great meal and I am miserable when I feel deprived of both, so I refuse to diet. Now, this doesn't mean I go around eating and drinking up the whole world. I'm a woman of a certain age and have to be mindful. But it does mean pick your spots. Eat well eighty percent of the time and 'blow your diet' twenty percent of the time.

I'm going to press pause here and talk for a bit about movement. I heard someone say sitting is the new smoking and I believe it. Our bodies need to walk, run, sweat, and stretch. It's non-negotiable. I know for sure that the fountain of youth lies there. I feel and look better when I work out. You don't have to be a marathon runner, Olympic gymnast, Orange Theory enthusiast or even a Peloton cult member. But find something you like to do that incorporates moving your body. Take regular walks. Try yoga or Pilates. Build up to running a 5k. Do something!

C) Surround yourself with people who glow. The world can be a very dark place, especially now when it feels like everything and everybody is out to get us. It can be very easy to fall down the rabbit holes of anger and despair. If you don't have a game plan to combat that, you'll never have peace.

Who are your friends? Do they bring joy and light or negativity and darkness? Have you spent any time thinking about that? There are some folks who can suck the life out of you like an emotional vampire. You feel it after you've spent any amount of time engaging with them. Cull through your mental rolodex of friendships and delete those that don't bring you joy. I know that may sound harsh, but sometimes it's you or them. And I'm going to choose myself every time.

I'm an empath and can usually read people's energy within a few minutes of meeting them. For me, there are three categories. Warm – the energy is positive, upbeat, cheerful, and nonjudgmental. These people are a vibe all by themselves and you can feel their joy. Dark – the energy is negative, sad, and traumatized. Something has happened to these people and they can't see their own beauty and light. Neutral – the energy can go either way depending on the moment and mood. I'll engage these people a few times to sort out where they fall. But if the energy goes negative, it's a no for me.

I am so fortunate to have people in my life who fall into the first category! They are light, joyful, funny, and interesting. We've had great conversations on everything from politics to celebrity crushes. In the spirit of spreading our light and joy, I've started cultivating a space that brings them together. I call this group The Lovelies and our events focus on joy, hope, love, and peace.

I hosted my first Lovelies event on March 29, 2025 – exactly one year to the day I left my CEO role. I hadn't planned it that way. This just happened to be the date that worked best for me based on my schedule. But we know how God works, right? And the gathering was everything I'd hoped it would be.

I asked the Lovelies to read Tia Williams' book Seven Days in June, which is a love story that involves family history, overcoming trauma and the soul-shaking impact someone can have on your life, even in a short period of time. Every one of the Lovelies has impacted my life in a positive way and I wanted to bring them together.

And again, we had a time! Over good food, drinks, and great conversation, we shared our own stories of love, perseverance, and joy. There was so much laughter in the room. Sitting there, surrounded by people I love, respect, and admire, was soul-satisfying because we shared our light. I plan to cultivate these gatherings quarterly because I need community and connection, now more than ever.

D)   Walk in Beauty – While on sabbatical, my husband and I have binged some great television shows. One of my favorites is Dark Winds, starring Zahn McClarnon. It's described as a psychological thriller that follows three Navajo Tribal Police officers, Joe Leaphorn, Bernadette Manuelito, and Jim Chee, in the 1970s rural, American Southwest. Think reservation land. Dry, remote, and starkly beautiful.

The show features a mostly native American cast. I know television series and movies rarely capture diverse, cultural communities well. And there will always be arguments about authenticity, but for me, this show gives a compelling glimpse of Native American culture with its rituals, spiritual connections to the land, pride, and sense of order.

During an episode, one characters tells another to 'Walk in Beauty.' I had never heard that term, but it resonated with me. So,

I looked it up. It is a Navajo concept called Hózhó that encourages living a balanced and harmonious way of life that is focused on physical, mental, emotional, and spiritual well-being. It emphasizes a deep connection to the natural world, understanding its wisdom and seeking to live in harmony with it.

Obviously, I'm not Navajo, but I can still rely on this principal to live a joy filled life. For me, it's about being cognizant of how you interact with people and the world. Understanding your place within the world. Serving and caring for others, being kind, spreading peace and light instead of sowing hate and destruction. It means finding harmony with the world and others.

This way of thinking has ushered in a new soft era for me. I'm not angry all the time. Disappointed and concerned about the state of the world, yes. Mad and ready to snap off at the slightest provocation, no. I look at my life and know it is very privileged and a blessing. To constantly complain and walk in anger would be an insult to God and all He's done for me.

I'm even re-thinking my personal brand. In the past, I've rocked power colors. Red, black, and gold. But now, I'm leaning toward pastels that are light and more joyful. What could be more powerful than owning your light and sharing it with other people to help them shine?

So, in writing this chapter, I am publicly apologizing to the elderly white woman at the Art Institute that was on the receiving end of negative energy from an over-worked and stressed-out Darlene. I am better now. I am healing. And I've chosen to walk in beauty.

Questions to Consider:

How are you taking care of yourself? Do you cultivate joy in your life?

_____

_____

_____

_____

_____

_____

_____

_____

Think about your friends. Are there a few friendships and people that you need to let go of because they drag your spirit down?

_____

_____

_____

_____

_____

_____

_____

_____

What are the narratives you tell yourself about work? Are they focused on grinding and hustling hard? Consider who benefits from that and who suffers.

_____

_____

_____

_____

_____

_____

_____

_____

_____

_____

Chapter Nine
One Life to Live

Oprah introduced me to my husband. Well, let me clarify that with a story. I have known Larry since the mid-1990s when I was a new lawyer and newly married. He is a financial planner and had come to meet with a group of young twenty-somethings to talk about investments and saving for our futures.

I don't remember that first meeting, but Larry says he does. I was running late and had breezed into the meeting after it had already started. Larry noticed me right away and thought I was cute. "Who is that?" he said to himself. But his professionalism and the fact that both of us were married to different people at the time, led us to have a strictly professional relationship.

Fast forward to 2008. I was recently divorced with a nine-year-old daughter and needed to think about my financial future, given the changes in my life circumstances. I scheduled a lunch meeting with Larry.

A few weeks before that meeting, I sat in my office taking a break from work – also known as tricking off. I was on Oprah's website scrolling through a list of upcoming shows when I saw they were looking for audience members on an upcoming show about love and the newly released movie 28 Dresses. I wrote up something about being recently divorced and sent the email. Much to my surprise, a few days later, one of Oprah's producers reached out to tell me I'd be a member of the audience! *How cool is that?* I thought. I'd driven past Oprah's studio countless times because it was in the same neighborhood as my former beautician.

Oh, you couldn't tell me nothing! I, Darlene Oliver, was going to be in the audience for a taping of the Oprah Winfrey Show! I got my hair done and picked out a cool outfit. When I got to the studio, I realized I wasn't going through the same doors as the other audience members. I had 'special instructions' that led me and my best friend Sylvia to a side entrance and a green room. I wouldn't just be in the audience. I'd be in the front row with four other women. This meant we got the full green room experience with make-up and a meet and great with Oprah. "Holy shit, I'm famous!" was my understandable response.

The show was all about the 28 Dresses movie and finding love. Kathryn Heigl was the guest that day. She was a lovely woman and visibly nervous during the taping – I mean; she was on the Oprah show! I sat in the front row all dolled up with my newly applied Oprah makeup, just happy for the experience. I don't remember everything that happened that day, but I do remember loving the commercial breaks when Oprah talked to the audience.

During one break, she jokingly took us women in the audience to task for what I'll call our 'dating efforts.' "All of y'all have these long lists of what you're looking for in a man. He's got to be so tall, look like this, have this. Expand your thinking. You could miss out on someone who doesn't meet everything you have on your long list. Expand your circle."

I thought about Oprah and her advice when I met with Larry for lunch a few weeks later. I'd known him for more than a decade. He seemed nice enough. Professional, handsome, a good guy. But I never thought about dating him. He was my financial advisor and more than a decade older than me. Our previous conversations had always been strictly professional. Then we went to lunch.

I couldn't believe it! We talked and laughed for two hours, literally closing the restaurant down. Larry opened up and shared a side of himself that I had never seen in all of our prior meetings. He was funny and engaging. He was kind. I left lunch thinking, 'that old man is hitting on me.' And he was in his own way.

A few weeks later, he invited me to his house and cooked me dinner. When I showed up, he was wearing a chef jacket and chef hat. He had a chef hat for me too and I sat on a stool in the kitchen, wearing my hat, watching him cook lamb chops and tell jokes. It was the best date I've ever had in my life.

We've been married for nearly a decade now and it has been an adventure. World traveling to fun and sometimes exotic places like Egypt, tasting menu meals in Paris, food and drink tours in Puerto Vallarta (one of our happy places), bourbon tastings in Kentucky, trips to the Harley Davidson Museum in Wisconsin.

Larry is my confidante, cheerleader, God-fearing voice of reason, and comedian. He is the person who pushes me to keep going when I want to give up. The man who makes me believe there's nothing I can't do and challenges me to get out there and do it.

But I could have easily missed out on the blessing that he is if I'd stuck to my 'must haves' list because I hadn't included 'date an older man' on it. Oprah was right. We can miss out on blessings when we hold on too tightly to our lists of 'must haves.' We need to expand our thinking and open ourselves up to wider possibilities. I don't want to miss the flight because I'm waiting on the bus.

As I think about my sabbatical journey, that sentiment still holds true. I want to avoid a list of 'must haves' for my next opportunity because it could be something I never expected that takes my breath away and is everything I didn't know I needed but am so glad I have. Having said that, I am warming to the idea of a portfolio life.

During my sabbatical, I read a book called The Portfolio Life by Christina Wallace. In it, she argues we shouldn't put all of our eggs in one basket when pursuing a fulfilling and financially viable career and life. Like a financial portfolio, we should diversify our lives and get involved in a mix of things that keep us afloat financially and bring a sense of fulfillment.

My portfolio life would include a viable stream of income, which I'm trying to figure out as I'm writing this book, civic engagement activities and something creative. Those last two are a cinch. I am currently on four nonprofit boards – the ACLU of Illinois, the Illinois Public Health Institute, Allies for Community Business, and the City Colleges of Chicago. I love being politically and socially engaged. I love great conversations and working on things I care about. With this list of organizations, I am focused on public health, civil liberties, educational access, and support for small businesses. Even writing this list of focus areas brings me joy because I know the leaders who run these organizations are at the forefront of making things better for people.

The creative prong of my three-legged portfolio life is also coming together nicely. When I tell you writing has become one of the biggest joys of my life, I mean it. I am literally giddy crafting a story, developing characters, writing love scenes, and sharing my first drafts with friends. I want my stories to be light, fun, inspiring, and funny. This isn't War and Peace. It's hot summer reads with love, sizzle, a sprinkle of social commentary and happily-ever-afters. Couldn't we all use more of that?

Writing this book has also been a blast. It's given me a chance to reflect on my sabbatical year and hopefully encourage people to lead happier, more fulfilling lives. The happier we all are, the less darkness can spread because our light snuffs it out. So, be on the lookout for my first novel Twin Flames: A Sutherland Love Story and the second book in the series, This is a Man's World: A Sutherland Love Story. I hope the joy I felt writing them leaps off of each page.

The income source has been more difficult to pin down. The predictable thing to do would be to secure another full-time job – most likely a leadership position in the nonprofit sector, where I've worked for more than a decade. The perceived stability of that is appealing. Regular paychecks, 401ks and health benefits are all vitally important. But as I wrote above, stability is illusive, despite the fact that our souls crave it. And if I am honest, the thought of going back to a high pressured, 9 to 5 (6,7 or 8) job doesn't make my heart sing. It kind of makes me sad and feels like I would have wasted the key learnings I've had during my sabbatical. Harriet never rushed back to the plantation unless she was bringing others to freedom.

As a middle-ground, I started my own consulting practice – Think and Do LLC. I provide strategic planning, workshop facilitation, interim executive director and coaching services for nonprofit organizations and leaders. Now, let me be clear, I've never seen myself as an entrepreneur. My mind doesn't think in terms of business jargon, marketing plans or finance. But it feels like I need to do it for now to have the flexibility I want so I can pursue the other two sides of my portfolio life. It's hard to be deeply creative and give your all to civic causes while holding down a sixty-hours a week, full-time job. Plus, I am deeply steeped in the nonprofit sector. Mission-driven work is in my DNA and I want to help these organizations thrive through consulting.

So, when I think about the work I'll do in the future, I am going to expand on the advice Oprah gave me nearly twenty years ago. Think bigger. Expand your circle. Open yourself up to something you never expected. I found my husband that way. Surely an exciting and joy filled opportunity can't be far behind. I just need to open myself up to the possibilities.

Questions to Consider:

What's on your list of 'must haves' for your career, mate, and life? Why and what might you be missing?

_____

_____

_____

_____

_____

_____

_____

_____

_____

What does your portfolio life look like? Are you engaged in any creative or service-related pursuits? Have you considered it?

_____

_____

_____

_____

_____

_____

_____

_____

Chapter Ten
Why Not You?

I've met President Barack Obama twice. Both encounters happened when he ran for the U.S. Senate in 2004. Back then, I worked for Robinson Curley & Clayton (RCC), a small civil rights litigation firm. Fay Clayton, one of the named partners, had known and worked with then candidate Obama for years at another firm and she was a big supporter for his Senate campaign. Backing him caused a bit of tension in the office because Ellen Robinson, also a named partner for the firm, had put her time and money behind rival Democratic candidate Daniel Hynes for the same Senate seat. Despite that, Fay insisted on doing a fundraiser for Obama at the firm's office.

Not one to miss out on supporting a Black candidate, I was firmly in the Obama camp and helped Fay organize the fundraiser. Let's set the context here. RCC had liberal lawyers who worked on civil rights cases for plaintiffs. Fay Clayton had argued a reproductive rights case before the United States Supreme Court and won 9 to 0. These were my kind of people –smart, civically engaged, and liberal leaning, but I was the only Black lawyer in the firm.

I remember the day of the fundraiser like it was yesterday. I had never heard Obama address a crowd, and this was before his big speech at the 2004 Democratic National Convention, so I was eager to hear what he had to say. On the day of the fundraiser, we'd packed the conference room with would be supporters. In breezed the future U.S. Senator and President of the United States – just as tall and good looking as he is on TV, but he was much younger then at forty-three.

I don't remember all the details of what he said to the crowd, but I do remember how I felt. I didn't quite swoon, but I was persuaded. Here was an incredibly smart Black man with inspiring ideas about how he could serve Illinois residents in Congress. By then, he had already won three terms in the Illinois State Senate. He was seasoned, qualified, and a dreamer focused on the things that brought us together as a nation instead of the easily identifiable things that could tear us apart.

After he gave his talk to the crowd at the firm and shook a few hands, I introduced myself. We were two of only three Black people in the room, after all.

"What are you doing here?" He asked with the infamous smile and a slightly skeptical look. "I work with Fay and I'm part of her fundraising group for your campaign," I said. His skepticism lingered. "You should be connected with a younger group of supporters. You know, some young Black folks. Let me introduce you to someone on my staff and we can get you connected." Of course, I agreed and I also wrote him a modest check to support the campaign. Little did I know I was talking to the future President of the United States!

The second time I met him was unexpected and much more casual. In the summer of 2004, I was on the board for the Chicago Foundation for Women (CFW) and we hosted a 'friend raiser' at the home of Martin "Marty" Nesbitt and Dr. Anita Blanchard. We had hoped to lure Dr. Blanchard onto the board and asking her to host a CFW event to learn more about the foundation was the first step.

She and her husband Marty had a beautiful home in the Kenwood neighborhood in Chicago. It was perfect for the event and Dr. Blanchard was an amazing host. The event was successful, with a great turnout and inspiring conversations about CFW's work.

As we wrapped things up, in walked U.S. Senate candidate Barack Obama. Walk is probably the wrong word. Saunter is more appropriate. I didn't know it then, but he and our forever first lady Michelle Obama were very good friends with Marty Nesbit and Dr. Blanchard. Obama wasn't at their house to campaign or fundraise. He'd dropped by just to see his friends and probably to relax. He looked tired. His tie had slid down a few notches and his shirt was unbuttoned at the top. His right hand was in his pocket as he made his way across the foyer to grab some leftover snacks from the CFW event.

I swallowed my surprise and checked my inner fan girl before walking over and re-introducing myself. Once I said the name Fay Clayton and reminded him of the fundraiser at my firm, he remembered me. "Good to see you. Did you ever get connected to another group?" I hadn't, but I did get to know the staff person he'd introduced me to and we went out to lunch a few times. I told him that. We chatted for a few more minutes and then he nicely excused himself, presumably to find his friends and take a well-deserved break from the campaign trail.

Mere months later, Obama delivered one of the most riveting speeches on the floor of the Democratic National Convention that I'd ever heard. In August 2004, he hadn't won the U.S. Senate seat yet and was still on the campaign trail for the election in the fall. I remember the excitement and thrumming in my chest as he talked about discarding the notion of separate red states and blue states and instead focusing on "these United States of America." I remember being inspired by this young, beautiful, and brilliant Black man who was a breath of fresh air – not only to the Democratic Party, but to our country. Obama represented positive change for people who are disregarded and left out of the American Dream. During that DNC speech, hope and possibility draped around his shoulders like Joseph's technicolor dream coat.

Those were such inspiring and hopeful times. And the eight years of his presidency between 2008 and 2016 felt incredibly optimistic, like anything was possible. As a Black person, I could breathe easier knowing that a thoughtful and caring Black man was in charge. He was someone who understood the challenges of being a person of color trying to make things happen in a country that was never built for your success. He knew what it was like to be raised by a single mother from meager means. He also knew the power of education and how it could change the trajectory of a person's life. President Obama had lived all of that and I could relate because I had as well.

As we slide into the chaos of 2025 with the notion of red and blue states at the center of the current administration's divisive policies, I long for the days of the Obama Presidency. Some called him a dreamer. Others argued he wasn't liberal or left leaning enough and he should have done more for people of color in America.

I'm not in that latter camp at all. That a Black man with a biological father from Kenya and a single, white mother from Kansas, who came from humble beginnings could become the President of the United States is a miracle. To date, there have been 46 presidents and Barack Obama is the only Black man who has ever claimed his place among them. This is both disheartening and incredible at the same time.

As I wind down my sabbatical, I've thought a lot about Obama's presidency. What gave him the audacity to believe he could not only be a U.S. Senator, but President of the United States? Where was his blueprint? Who told him it was okay to dream that big and where does that self-belief come from? There were so many times along the campaign trail when he could have counted himself out. Fourteen other Democrats ran against him in the Senate primary. He beat them all. The Republican party put its own Black, male candidate up to run against him for the Senate. Obama beat him too.

In the race for President, he endured the naysayers and veiled racism that said he should step aside and let rival candidate Hillary Clinton claim the Democratic nomination for President. In his unflappable, swag-infused way, Obama brushed aside all of that swirling doubt and pushback. He persisted in his cause and ultimately won both hotly contested races for President.

Recently, I looked at the 2008 election results. Obama won because Black, Hispanic and Asian voters overwhelmingly voted for him. Yes, some white voters pulled the lever for him too, but most voted for Republican candidate John McCain. Obama won because he built a coalition of support across race.

I was so inspired by Obama's unlikely rise to political prominence that my first fiction book, Twin Flames, focuses on Shelby Reynolds, who helps her mentor and family friend Senator Cyrus Banks on his campaign to become the first Black President of the United States. Of course, there is a lot of tension, misunderstandings, and drama along the way, but my Obama-like character, Cyrus Banks, plays a key role in the book.

As I wrote Twin Flames, I kept thinking that we all need that Obama "Why Not Me?" spirit in every aspect of our lives. It's that inner belief that things might look impossible, but we're going to try anyway. It might not turn out as we hoped, but we'll still give it a shot. Why take ourselves out of the game before its even started?

Sadly, most of us don't think like that. We count ourselves out of opportunities all the time. We doubt our experience and our worth. We downplay our credentials and come up with a list of reasons why that job, that fellowship, that potential mate won't work out for us.

I did the same thing as I applied for jobs again. I asked myself: "Was I really qualified for that new role?" "Does my experience translate into what the organization says it wants?" "Maybe I'm not a good fit," I said to myself.

I also questioned myself as I looked for a literary agent for my romance novel series. "I know they get so many queries. Is mine strong enough to get their attention?" "Is my writing solid enough for an agent to want to represent me?"

But once again, I had to check myself. I've been blessed with an embarrassment of riches in professional experience. My resume is filled with amazing achievements. I've also written many Op-ed pieces and articles deemed worthy enough for publication.

I realized that sometimes we need to remind ourselves of who we are and whose we are. I'm not a novice to work. I've thrived in many diverse, professional environments. I have great contacts and friends. I have a heart for service and a mind to do great things. I can tell an interesting story with loveable characters that people want to read about.

The holy spirit dwells in me. I am strong and courageous. Any organization would be lucky to have my gifts and talents. I mean, come on! I've even met the President of the United States twice! And like him, I've decided I'm going to saunter into every interview and agent pitch oozing with confidence and swagger. I will take up space and declare – "Why Not Me!" If Barack Hussein Obama could live out his dreams, push aside all doubts and make the impossible possible, why can't Darlene Oliver Hightower do the same? Why can't you?

Questions to Consider:

Have there been times when you've missed out on opportunities because of self-doubt? Why did you question yourself?

_____

_____

_____

_____

_____

_____

_____

_____

Do you know people who have overcome great odds and found a way to thrive? Are there similarities between them and you?

_____

_____

_____

_____

_____

_____

_____

_____

THE PLOT TWIST

What is the biggest dream you've ever had for yourself? Have you taken steps to achieve it? Why or why not?

_____

_____

_____

_____

_____

_____

_____

_____

Chapter Eleven
Ready, Set, Go!

In January 2025, I sat in church, worried. My savings had dwindled, and I'd gone nearly a year without a paycheck. My husband, bless his heart, was still super supportive. But I was antsy. "Come on God, I just know you haven't brought me this far to only bring me this far," I thought while sitting in the pew. I'd applied for jobs, done interviews, and had one- on-ones with nearly my entire network. My goal was to firm up an opportunity by the end of the first quarter in 2025. But nothing was waiting in the wings for me. What was my next thing? How could I make money? Especially when I had only about ten years left before retirement. I needed to get back on track with a new job so I could start saving again.

So, just like the fall of 2023, during the altar call at church, I closed my eyes, clasped my hands in prayer, and called out to God for direction and guidance. I consider myself a force for good with a desire to invest in people and my community. I was softer and more balanced now but still impact driven. Surely God had a new message and assignment for me.

As I stood there laying out my hopes and the desires of my heart to God, the holy spirit whispered to me again and said – "You don't know HOW God is going to bless you!" And the meaning of that was like – stand back and watch God work! Find peace in knowing everything you need is already in your hands or on its way. God is about to show up and show out!

That's when I realized this year hasn't been about finding my next job. I have spent my entire career trying to transform and improve the lives of others. God has spent this year transforming me. Drawing me nearer to Him. Pushing me to deepen my relationship with Him by walking by faith. I've literally had "Walk by Faith" tattooed on my left foot for over five years, but before my plot twist, I don't think I ever truly lived it.

My sabbatical has taught me the real value of those words. This has been a faith walk, which means I have to learn to surrender and have faith that things will work themselves out. I am being called to walk in the spirit and to live my life more freely, by faith. I have to trust that God will get me where I need to go; that there is a plan for my life and I don't have to work myself to death to make it happen. Knowing that, my spirit is calmer and I have so much more peace and joy.

I've also learned a lot about myself in the past year. I don't need the co-sign, approval, or applause of other people. I don't need everyone to understand me. Instead, I choose to do what is in my own heart, because that's where God is. That's where love is and where purpose is.

I also think I spent the earlier part of my sabbatical year looking for something outside of me for comfort and joy. But that peace, that comfort, has been inside of me all along. No job, trip, club, person, or relationship can give me peace or purpose. I need to look within myself to find it and then polish it every day. I have to do the heart work, not the hard work.

I've also realized that our job is to become more of who we truly are every day. To use our energy to get to our true selves and work on being the best people we can be. This means I am now very selective about how I spend my time and who I spend it with. If it's not bringing me joy, peace, and light, I don't want it. My relationships, work and activities should all bring out the best in me. They should feed me light and life.

In February 2025, I started a new devotional journal called 100 Days of Believing Bigger by Marshawn Evans Daniels. One of my dear friends gave it to me after a night out of food and fellowship. "Girl, I've got something that I think you'll really enjoy," my friend Abosede said. "I've been reading this journal and it's fantastic. Take a look and tell me what you think."

I'd never heard of Ms. Daniels, or her devotional, but let me tell you, it has been life changing. There are so any gems and insights about living your life from a forward-thinking and bigger perspective – refusing to limit what God has in store for you. I have dog-eared pages and notes written all over the book. Whenever I got down about my circumstances or felt overwhelmed by the unknown, Ms. Daniels's words got me back on track. And I mean literally snatched me back to God's light and purpose. These are just a few of the passages that I've underlined and refer to often:

> He desires that you love who you are and grow to operate with supernatural courage using the gifts, personality, and intellect He gave you.

> You are a voice! We're created in His image—a living Word. God is voice and uses voice to create new ideas, miracles, and solutions....You don't just have a voice, you are voice...Your voice unlocks the greater purpose and possibility in others.

> God is more concerned with our character and capacity than He is our calling. We can become so obsessed with doing a work *for* God that we forget to become *who* God needs first.

> The pressure to do what we've always done, what we've always been taught, and what we've always seen can block us from discerning and entering the new God has for us...**Know that your next-level mission and calling aren't found in the past.** As you embrace God's new vision for you, you'll start seeing new pathways and doors open. (emphasis mine)

This last one has been a key lesson for me because of my 'only human' desire to return to what is familiar, like the jobs I've had in the past. On more than one occasion, the pre-sabbatical voice of reason in my head has said, "put your hat in the ring for that CEO job." Or "Maybe you should go back to RUSH, you did well there." Or "apply for that C-Suite position so you can start saving for retirement again." But Sabbatical Darlene pushes back on this thinking every time. I'd escaped the hamster wheel of overwork, stress, and grind culture. I can't turn back to that now. And I honestly believe that the more traditional nine-to-five route hasn't opened up for me because God wants me to live a bigger and bolder life. I did not come here to be ordinary. I came to be great.

And I have to acknowledge that when I am still and really tuning into myself, I feel the pull and urge to try something new. I have a sense that whatever is next for me won't be something I have done before. As suggested in my devotional recently, there are so many things that I *could do*, but what am I feeling *called to do*?

If I am honest, writing books feels like something I've been called to do. In a year's time, I've written two novels and this non-fiction book. The words have leapt onto the page. I haven't struggled with storylines, character development, ideas, or writer's block. I sat at my computer and the words came flying out like they've just been dying to get on the page. The stories, process and the outline for this book have come from somewhere deep inside of me without a lot of handwringing, wrestling or stress. I have to believe the source of this work is divine because of how freely it has come.

During this sabbatical year, I am learning that my purpose may be to help people live more bold, vibrant, joyful, and faith-filled lives. I've always wanted to serve my community and help people. I hope this book does just that by asking you to take the time to reevaluate what is important to you and live a more joyful, fulfilling life.

The goal of my romance novels is to provide a fun and light escape. To bring some joy and laughter to a world that could certainly use more love. The goal of this book is to get you to reexamine what really matters and take the bold step of creating a life that is more fulfilling. I don't want to be the only light out here shining. I need you to join me. That's why I can see myself writing more books and doing speaking engagements to encourage others to live out their wildest dreams.

And what about you? You've taken the time to read eleven chapters of this book. What is the plot twist in your own life? I know not everyone has the luxury of taking off a full year from work, or even several months, but are there ways you can create space in your own life to pursue the things that matter? Can you stay present and focus on your people? Dive into something Uber creative? Maybe you pause for a week or two while on vacation and ask yourself some really hard questions. Maybe you spend that time coming up with a plan (or even a few baby steps) to help you live a life that is more fulfilling.

Your Plot Twist

Here are a few questions to ask yourself:

It's Sunday night. How are you feeling about going into the office on Monday? Is there a sense of dread? Anxiety? Ask yourself why and if there are things you can do to change that, even if they are small tweaks.

Look at your calendar for the week. Is there any time on it for rest, play and wonder? Or are you literally in back-to-back meetings? Why is that? How can you give yourself more time to breathe – even if it's just making sure you have at least a ten-minute break between your meetings?

Is your work in line with your personal values? Work is more fulfilling when it aligns with who you are. Consider purchasing One Core Value cards (https://bestself.co/products/core-values-deck) to help zero in on what really matters to you. And then use those values when you think about your work and personal life. My three core values are community, service, and justice, and I use them as guides when choosing opportunities and projects.

What brings you joy? Have you been intentional in surrounding yourself with people and activities that are fun that you know you'll enjoy? I mentally track the time between waking up and laughing at something funny my husband has said. Those joy breaks throughout the day can be game changers.

THE PLOT TWIST

Do you spend any time during the day or the week in quiet reflection? This could be prayer, meditation, reading or anything that allows you space and time to be still. Stillness is a value and we should practice it every day to have a fuller life.

What would you do if you had more time? I'm sure working more would not be on your list. How can you thread things into your life that you've 'always been meaning to do?'

Are you happy with your life right now? If the answer is no, why not and what can you do to put yourself on the road to a happier, healthier, more joy-filled life?

CONCLUSION

It is May 2025 as I write this. I've applied for three opportunities that I am excited about. One is a role with a food insecurity focused organization; another is a position in a workforce development focused non-profit; and the last one is leading a small foundation. These positions would provide a balanced, portfolio life. I would still do impactful work without sacrificing my health, joy, and sanity. I would still have time to write! I hope that I'll be selected for one of these great opportunities. But even if that doesn't happen, I'm fine trusting God's timing.

I am looking for a literary agent and have sent out over thirty pitch letters. I'm convinced that someone will fall in love with my characters in Twin Flames and help me secure a publishing deal…. because, why not! I can envision myself doing talks in Chicago and beyond about the Plot Twist and what I learned on my sabbatical. I see myself on stage, doing panel discussions and encouraging people to live their best lives. Most importantly, I see me living out my dreams and becoming the best version of myself. All of my past challenges, disappointments, triumphs and 'aha' moments have led me to this place of wide open, vast opportunity. And I can't wait to see what God has next for me!

Acknowledgements

Writing this book has been a group effort, and I'm so thankful to everyone who has helped me along the way. My first thank you is to my family. My mother Ramona laid such a great foundation for me. Her focus on the importance of education changed the trajectory of my life and opened so many doors. I am grateful for her.

I dedicated this book to my husband Larry, but I want to acknowledge him again here. Thank you for being such a strong supporter of my big ideas and dreams. You don't just say you love me; you show up and support me every single day. I deeply appreciate your love, humor, and partnership.

To my daughter Sydni who has grown up to be such a compassionate and beautiful young woman. I cherish our relationship and friendship. You are my greatest accomplishment! And you keep me laughing and young!

To my bestie Sylvia. We've been friends for nearly forty years (which is a miracle because we're both twenty-five in our heads!) You are always down for tomfoolery and shenanigans! Thank you for your humor and kindness. You are and will always be sunshine.

There are so many friends, acquaintances, colleagues, fellow board members, trustees and mentors that have been an invaluable help to me along my career journey. They are too numerous to list. But a special shout out to every leader in the Black Women CEOs group, the Lovelies, my former staff and colleagues at Rush and West Side United. I want to especially acknowledge Dr. David Ansell, who was not only my mentor at Rush, but my sponsor and always pushed me to grow professionally. We made a great team! A special shout out to the twenty-five social justice leaders across the country that I interviewed during my Chicago Community Trust fellowship. I have never felt so inspired in my life. Most of them are still doing the work. Thank God for their courage and perseverance!

Special shoutouts to everyone who helped put this book together: Patrick Oliver for guiding me through the publishing process; Khia Ancalade from Khia's Canvas, who designed the beautiful front and back covers of the book. My editor, Jadi Z. Omowale, whose feedback on the draft was so positive! Relana Johnson for the book design and layout and Dr. David Ansell, Professor Jacqueline Stewart, and CEO leader Nicole Robinson for reading early chapters of the book and providing endorsements.

And finally, thank you for taking the time to read this book. I hope you found something funny and inspiring that you could relate to. I really believe we are all masterpieces, and it is our job to live up to that every day. I hope the Plot Twist helped you, at least in some small way, on your journey of reflection, rest, and rejuvenation.

Endnotes

1   For a detailed personal account of patient care and outcomes at Cook County Hospital, *County, Life, Death, and Politics at Chicago's Public Hospital,* by my old boss Dr. David Ansell is an interesting read.

2   Thrive as They Lead, Advancing the Infrastructure to Support Black Women leaders in the D.C. Metro Area Nonprofit Sector, Washington Area Women's Foundation, October 2023.